# Language and Technology

The INTERTEXT series has been specifically designed to meet the needs of contemporary English Language Studies. *Working with Texts: A core introduction to language analysis* (3rd edn, 2008) is the foundation text, which is complemented by a range of 'satellite' titles. These provide students with hands-on practical experience of textual analysis through special topics, and can be used individually or in conjunction with *Working with Texts*.

This accessible textbook in the Routledge INTERTEXT series offers students hands-on practical experience of textual analysis focused on language and technology. Written in a clear, user-friendly style, it combines practical activities with texts, accompanied by commentaries and suggestions for further study.

Aimed at A-Level and beginning undergraduate students, *Language and Technology*:

- explores the history of new communication tools such as texting, Facebook and online forums
- examines the public discourses about these new tools
- incorporates real texts such as adverts, newspaper articles and chat-room data
- includes a comprehensive glossary of terms.

**Angela Goddard** is Professor of English Language and Head of Subject for Languages and Linguistics at York St John University, UK. She is Chair of English Language for a national examination board.

**Beverly Geesin** is Senior Lecturer and Head of Programme for Communication and Culture at York St John University, UK.

## The Intertext series

The Routledge INTERTEXT series will develop readers' understanding of how texts work. It does this by showing some of the designs and patterns in the language from which they are made, by placing texts within the contexts in which they occur, and by exploring relationships between them.

The series consists of a foundation text, *Working with Texts: A core introduction to language analysis*, which looks at language aspects essential for the analysis of texts, and a range of satellite texts. These apply aspects of language to a particular topic area in more detail. They complement the core text and can also be used alone, providing the user has the foundation skills furnished by the core text.

### Benefits of using this series:

◎ **Unique** – written by a team of respected teachers and practitioners whose ideas and activities have also been trialled independently.

◎ **Multi-disciplinary** – provides a foundation for the analysis of texts, supporting students who want to achieve a detailed focus on language.

◎ **Accessible** – no previous knowledge of language analysis is assumed, just an interest in language use.

◎ **Comprehensive** – wide coverage of different genres: literary texts, notes, signs, advertisements, leaflets, speeches, conversation.

◎ **Student-friendly** – contains suggestions for further reading; activities relating to texts studied; commentaries after activities; key terms highlighted and an index of terms.

**The series editors:**

**Adrian Beard** lectures in English Language and Linguistics at York St John University and is a Chief Examiner for AS- and A-Level English Literature. He has written extensively on the subjects of literature and language, and his publications include *Texts and Contexts* (Routledge) and *The Language of Sport*, *The Language of Politics* and *Language Change* in this series.

**Angela Goddard** is Head of Subject for Languages and Linguistics at York St John University. Her publications include *The Language of Advertising* and *Language and Gender* in this series. Her current research interests are in aspects of identity and language use in computer-mediated communication. She is Chair of Examiners for English Language A-Level at a major national exam board.

**Core textbook:**

*Working with Texts: A core introduction to language analysis* (3rd edn; 2007)
Ronald Carter, Angela Goddard, Danuta Reah, Keith Sanger, Nikki Swift

**Satellite titles:**

*Language and Gender*
(2nd edn)
Angela Goddard and Lindsey Meân

*The Language of Advertising:*
*Written texts*
(2nd edn)
Angela Goddard

*The Language of Newspapers*
(2nd edn)
Danuta Reah

*Language Change*
Adrian Beard

*The Language of Children*
Julia Gillen

*The Language of Comics*
Mario Saraceni

*Language and Region*
Joan C. Beal

*The Language of Science*
Carol Reeves

*The Language of Conversation*
Francesca Pridham

*The Language of Speech and*
*Writing*
Sandra Cornbleet and Ronald Carter

*The Language of Drama*
Keith Sanger

*The Language of Television*
Jill Marshall and Angela Werndly

*The Language of War*
Steve Thorne

*The Language of ICT: Infromation and*
*Communication Technology*
Tim Shortis

*The Language of Websites*
Mark Boardman

*The Language of Magazines*
Linda McLoughlin

*The Language of Work*
Almut Koester

*The Language of Politics*
Adrian Beard

*The Language of Sport*
Adrian Beard

*The Language of Poetry*
John McRae

*The Language of Humour*
Alison Ross

*The Language of Fiction*
Keith Sanger

# Language and Technology

◎ Angela Goddard
◎ Beverly Geesin

## Routledge
Taylor & Francis Group

LONDON AND NEW YORK

First edition published 2011
by Routledge
2 Park Square, Milton Park, Abingdon, Oxon, OX14 4RN

Simultaneously published in the USA and Canada
by Routledge
711 Third Avenue, New York, NY 10017

*Routledge is an imprint of the Taylor & Francis Group, an informa business*

*British Library Cataloguing in Publication Data*
A catalogue record for this book is available from the British Library

*Library of Congress Cataloging in Publication Data*
Goddard, Angela.
  Language and technology/Angela Goddard and Beverly Geesin.
  – 1st ed.
  p. cm.
  Includes bibliographical references.
  1. Communication and technology.  2. Language and languages –
Study and teaching – Technological innovations.  3. Social
networks.  4. Interpersonal relations.  I. Geesin, Beverly.
  II. Title.
  P96.T42G63 2011
  006.7'54 – dc22                               2010046816

ISBN: 978-0-415-60416-1 (pbk)

Typeset in Stone Sans and Stone Serif
by Florence Production Ltd, Stoodleigh, Devon

MIX
Paper from
responsible sources
FSC
www.fsc.org  FSC® C004839

Printed and bound in Great Britain by the MPG Books Group

# contents

# acknowledgements

The publishers would like to thank:

Garner, R. (2005) 'English exam hit by epidemic of street language', *The Independent*, 17 September

*The Daily Mail* (2008) 'Oldest phone book rings up £87,000', 19 June

*Metro* (2005) 'Text mad children turning to drink', 17 February

*Metro* (2005) 'Texts cause "more harm than dope"', 22 April

*The Times*, 2008, 'Mobile phone image', 4 December

Cobra Facebook advert © Cobra, with permission.

The authors would like to thank the following for permission to use their material: Josie Beszant, Howard Brereton, Ruth Doyle, Megan Geesin, Lindsey Meân, Monika Mondor, Dinesh Vaswani, Stormy and Washington.

Every effort has been made to seek permission to reproduce copyright material before the book went to press. If any proper acknowledgement has not been made, we would invite copyright holders to inform us of the oversight.

Please note that all data is presented as it originally occurred.

# In the beginning: language and technology

## Aims of this unit

- To explore some initial definitions of 'technology'.
- To review some of the different communication technologies that you and others have learnt to manage.
- To analyse how new communication tools are marketed to us.
- To begin to think about some of the social issues raised by techno-logical developments in communication.

## Introduction: what is 'technology'?

The word 'technology' is derived from a Greek term, 'tekhna', meaning 'art' or 'craft'. (The 'logy' ending means 'study of' or 'application of', and might be familiar to you from other contemporary words such as psychology, sociology).

Although we might have quite narrowly scientific associations for the term 'technology', thinking perhaps of modern inventions such as the Dyson vacuum cleaner or the iPod, in theory any application of knowledge to create a system of some kind is included under this heading. By this definition, writing itself is a technology, as it is a systematic **representation** using symbols; and all those earlier writing implements and materials – from papyrus to slate and from quills to biros – were as 'hi-tech' and cutting edge to their users as our computer interfaces and touchscreens are to us.

Regardless of the historical time in question, technologies that are seen as 'new' appear to generate fear and anxiety along with the excitement that greets new discoveries. Where language is concerned, anxious responses to new linguistic forms have a long history. For example, the philosopher Plato, living in Greece in the fifth century BC, viewed writing with great suspicion, almost as a form of intellectual 'cheating':

> [Writing] will introduce forgetfulness into the soul of those who learn it: they will not practise using their memory because they will put their trust in writing, which is external and depends on signs that belong to others, instead of trying to remember from the inside, completely on their own. You have not discovered a potion for remembering, but for reminding; you provide your students with the appearance of wisdom, not with its reality. Your invention will enable them to hear many things without being properly taught, and they will imagine that they have came to know much while for the most part they will know nothing. And they will be difficult to get along with, since they will merely appear to be wise instead of really being so.
>
> (Hackforth, 1972: 275a–b)

Plato clearly saw knowledge as inextricably bound up with memory, so in his view the new technology of writing allowed thoughts to be stored elsewhere and therefore contributed to a kind of cognitive inertia. But there are perhaps some further reasons why the combination of language and technology might make people jittery.

The idea of new communication technologies may produce a particular level of anxiety because people have to learn new ways of expressing themselves and handling themselves socially, as well as new operational skills to manage the technology. For example, when the telephone was first marketed and popularly used, people had to be instructed how to hold the receiver but, perhaps more crucially, given advice about what words to use in order to begin and end a conversation politely and agreeably. See Text 1:1.

## Text 1:1 Oldest phone book

**Oldest phone book rings up £87,000**

The only known copy of the world's first telephone directory fetched £87,375 at auction in New York yesterday – four times more than expected.

Twenty pages long, it contains the names and numbers of 391 subscribers around New Haven, Connecticut, and was issued in 1878 – just two years after the invention of the phone by Alexander Graham Bell.

The directory contains some useful advice for inexperienced callers: 'Should you wish to speak to another subscriber, you should commence the conversation by saying 'Hulloa!'. When you are done talking say 'That is all'. The person spoken to should say 'ok'.

'While talking, always speak low and distinct, and let the telephone rest lightly against your upper lip, leaving the lower lip and jaw free'.

The book was bought by a private collector at the Christie's sale.

(Source: *Daily Mail*, 19 June 2008)

An 'older' technology, such as the landline phone, can of course be given a new lease of life and become a 'new' technology by being used in a new way. Below, on p. 4 (Text 1:2) is an image of an early mobile phone (called a 'cellphone' in the USA), which made the phone experience radically different from that associated with fixed-line communication. Looking at this phone now should act as a reminder that communication technologies are extremely fast-moving, so people will have very different experiences depending on their age and what counts as 'new' within their lifetime.

## Text 1:2 First mobile phone

**FIRST MOBILE PHONE**

The use of a form of mobile telephone (two-way radio) was pioneered by the Chicago police in the 1930s to stay ahead of Prohibition gangsters. The mobile as we know it was invented by Dr Martin Cooper of Motorola. It was first used in 1973 in a demonstration call, made by Cooper to his rival, Joel Engel, of Bell Laboratories.

Source: *The Times*, 11 October 2006

## Learning about technology

*Activity*

If you can do this activity in a group situation and with people of different ages, your results will be all the richer.

List as many examples as you can of the different forms of new communication you have learnt to use. Then try to recall the point in time when you first experienced any of them: for example, you may remember the first time you made a call on a mobile phone, sent an email or a 'Tweet', or wrote your first text, chatroom message or wall post on a social networking site.

What you recall as your first experience will depend on a range of factors, including not just the new forms of communication that have developed in your lifetime, but also the age at which your family thought it appropriate for you to have access to them.

What do you remember about your feelings towards the new technology at the time? Can you remember anything about the process of learning how to use the new tool, or how to behave in this new environment? For example, did you copy others in their behaviour, ask others for help, or read tips and guidelines? Did you try some 'test' runs in order to see how the new communication worked? Did you make many mistakes in your use? How do you think you came across to others in those early attempts to manage the new circumstances you were in?

(Note: there is a commentary on this activity at the back of the book.)

## The marketing of communication tools

Many of us have had to learn how to use new tools as adults, so we are often in a position similar to children acquiring skills for the first time. But now that the adult world is populated with many new 'gadgets', including tools for communication, it is predictable that toy companies have started to produce versions for children.

*Activity*

Look at the toy mobile phone adverts in Texts 1:3 and 1:4.

These two products represent a small sample of the available range, where different phones are aimed at children of different ages, often with intervals of six months or less.

- What strategies are the advertisers using in order to sell these toys?
- What claims are being made about the skills children learn by using these toys?
- What messages about the world are being communicated by these toys?

(Note: there is a commentary on this activity at the back of the book.)

## Text 1:3 My First Soft Mobile Phone

(front)                                    (back)

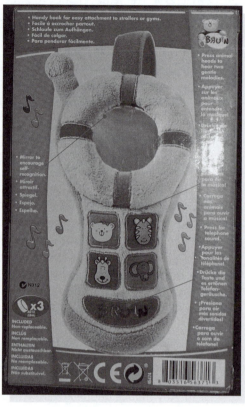

## Text 1:4 Leapfrog 'Chat & Count' cell phone

(front)                          (side: 'To be there every step of the way')

## Technology and surveillance

The toy phone advertisements you have been analysing promote the idea of children's language skills being developed by their use of communication tools. And yet there are public anxieties about who exactly our children might be communicating with, if we allow them free use of all the new media available to us. As a result, the same tools that cause anxiety

7

can also be used to monitor children's interactions more than ever before. The next part of this unit will help you to explore this rather complex situation, and to think about the implications for language and communication that result from such conflicting interests and concerns.

The activities below will involve you in scrutinising a number of different websites that either advertise products that are specifically designed for surveillance, or where surveillance might be an outcome of something that was designed for other purposes. Obviously, products and services in this area change rapidly, so the website that accompanies this text will offer updates to sites that are new and equivalent to the links provided here. In addition, where possible, sites will be glossed below so that, if the actual site in question is no longer available, you will know the type of generic product being described and will be able to find equivalents yourself.

## 'Communication' toys as surveillance: the Teddyfone

Aside from the toy mobile phones discussed above, there are functioning mobile phones that are marketed to children (or, more accurately, to parents to purchase for children) - for example, the Teddyfone (www. kiddyfone.com).

The focus for the marketing of this phone is security and it is described on the site as a 'specifically designed child safety phone'. It is in the shape of a bear and comes in the gender-specific colours of pink or blue. The phone only has four buttons, limiting the use to four pre-programmed phone numbers. It has no screen, no texting capability, no music and no games. Instead, the features on this phone are primarily focused towards the parent. This phone allows the parent to restrict who the child calls. It also has a tracking function that enables the parent to log into the system online and locate the phone (and, presumably, the child). Additionally, it has a function where the phone turns into a microphone and the parent can call in and hear what is going on around the child, essentially eavesdropping.

There are many more phones that are marketed with children as the notional consumers, but where parental concerns about children's safety are being targeted in the advertising copy. For example, Firefly ('The mobile phone for mobile kids') focuses on the idea of children's freedom and mobility – a positive message for child consumers, but a threatening idea for parents to cope with (www.fireflymobile.com).

## People-tracking: phone applications ('apps')

'Apps' is short for 'applications software' – programmes that are built for specific functions. Most recently, apps have featured in the context of mobile phone products that we can download from the internet to enable us to perform a wide range of different functions, including tracking the whereabouts of other people. For example, Family Tracker (www.logsat. com/iPhone/familytracker) suggests that others in your life might be up to no good – your husband might be having an affair rather than working late, your wife might be in bed with her personal trainer rather than being out with her friends, or your child might be partying instead of doing his homework. Family Tracker will enable you to 'find them out'.

## Internet surveillance: Net Nanny products

Parental monitoring is, of course, not limited to mobile phones. There is a large market for products that enable parents to monitor how their children interact online. These tools vary widely in terms of how much monitoring they enable. Some merely act as filters, restricting inappropriate websites such as ones with graphic images or pornography. Much of this can be done through software already on the computer. For instance, Apple computers all come with parental controls that can be set to restrict the use of certain applications, or access to certain websites. Like many other applications, they also allow parents to set up timers and to keep a log of how much time a particular user is online. These types of software enable parents to restrict web access, but without much prying into the specifics. To allow for greater monitoring, parents using the Apple parental controls or similar software can keep a log of every website visited. Or, more intrusively still, parents may access the actual transcripts of conversations online, every email, instant message or discussion board post.

There are also many commercial products that are specifically for managing young people's online interactions – for example, Net Nanny (www.netnanny.com) and BeNetSafe (www.benetsafe.com).

In order to sell these products, the associated advertising copy can deliberately play on parental anxieties about their children's safety online: for example, two former Symantec ads pictured innocent-looking young girls working on their computers while the advertising hooks warned of imminent dangers. In one ad, the girl's mother sits nearby reading a newspaper with the following headline facing outwards:

STALKERS could use the internet to contact your children.

**9**

In another, a girl plays on her computer while, behind her, her bedroom window opens to admit several threatening-looking characters, who are climbing through. The hook reads as follows, making a link between the metaphor of computer-based 'windows' and the real version:

Best to keep some windows closed.

(Symantec refused permission to reproduce these adverts here.)

*Activity*

Discuss the following questions:

• What (if any) techniques did the adults in your household use to control your electronic communication when you were young? Did you find ways to subvert their surveillance?
• Discuss the advantages and disadvantages of children having mobile phones. At what age do you think it is acceptable for children to have their own phones?
• The Teddyfone is very clearly a monitoring device, but any mobile phone can be used to trace the whereabouts of the phone's user. Should we be using this device for this purpose, in your view?
• Is it ever acceptable to eavesdrop on children's conversations? If you discovered that your parents could listen in to your phone conversations and access your text messages remotely, how would that make you feel? Would it change the way you interact with your friends? Would your language use be different? How would it change your relationship with your parents?

(Note: there is no commentary on this activity.)

## Extension activities

1    Collect some advertisements for products associated with new technologies (for example, computers, internet providers, mobile phones) and analyse their persuasive techniques. If you want a comparison, you could look at how the same kind of product (for example, mobile phones) is marketed to different audiences (for example, in women's magazines compared with men's) or via different media (for example, paper-based advertising compared with an online version).

2    Do some research in toy shops on children's toys that involve new technologies. For example, do toy shops in your area stock toy computers and mobile phones? If so, how are these toys represented? Are there assumptions about the age and gender of the child who might be the recipient of the toy? What language skills do the products claim children will learn, as a result of using their toys?

3    Research how children feel about the new communication tools that surround them. For example, do they or their friends have mobile phones? If so, how do they use them? Do their parents monitor their use of computers and, if so, how?

4    Interview people of different ages about their experiences of new technologies and communication. Write up your results and consider the extent to which your interviewees' accounts reveal similarities and differences in their experiences.

*Unit* two

# Communication repertoires and multimodality

## Aims of this unit

- To explore the range of communication tools that individuals might be using as part of their daily routines.
- To consider how different communities might vary in how communication tools are used.

### *Activity*

In Text 2:1, a 12-year-old American girl talks about how new technologies are integrated into her everyday life. Particularly, she discusses how important text messaging has become for her, even though she has only had a mobile phone for two months. How does this account compare with your own experiences?

(Text in brackets has been added for explanatory purposes.)

(Note: there is no commentary on this activity.)

13

## Text 2:1 A day in the life . . .

In second grade, I would play online with Webkinz (*an online game where users have virtual pets*). We would go on and take care of our pets and stuff. We would dress up their rooms, play games to get money. Your friends could come to your house but you couldn't type in the message. You could only put up pre-made messages like 'How are you?' It was fun but we didn't usually talk to each other.

In fifth grade I would talk to my friends on Skype. But not many have accounts. I usually talk to one friend because she lives in New Jersey, we just type (*use instant messaging*).

So the best way to reach my friends now, I would text them or call them. Probably call them. It depends on what I want. If I want to know if they want to come over here I'll call them. If I want to know what's for homework I'll text them. It's easier, I just text them and they text back the information. I mostly text people at least like once a day. I do a bunch on the weekend and not that many during the week because I see them. If I'm out somewhere and I'm doing something I don't really want to call them, I text. I can't call much because I don't have money. I don't have unlimited calling, just $20 credit a month.

I don't have a Facebook account. All of my friends do. I think they lie about their age. They talk to other people from school and stuff. I'll probably never have a Facebook account, that's what Mommy says.

*Activity*

### Desert island choices . . .

While doing the activity above, you will have noticed that the individual in question, in effect, made an inventory of all the pieces of technology that are (or were) part of her life. Now imagine that you have to make a choice between the tools you use, and you can only choose one of them – which aspect of technology would you choose, and why? In other words, which item has become so much a part of your existence that you'd find it hard to live without it? Compare your choice with that of others in your group, if you're working in a group situation.

(Note: there is no commentary on this activity.)

# The language of new communication tools

Above, you may have chosen an item that didn't necessarily involve your own communication – for example, an iPod. But as part of your thinking about your experiences more widely, you will most probably have considered several new communication tools that require you to choose a style of writing or speaking. In the last 20 years, we have added many different new **genres** of communication to the more traditional choices of face-to-face spoken communication and paper-based writing: for example, email, **txting (SMS)** and **social networking sites (SNS)**, to name but a few.

There is no single 'language of new technologies', but rather a range of styles of communication that share certain properties of language use. Each of us will vary our communication to suit the audience(s) we are addressing, but the nature of the medium is also important, and our sense of what it can do (or not).

A useful starting point for thinking about different communication tools is the idea of **constraints** (Sellen and Harper, 2001), which covers the **affordances** of the communication tool (i.e. what it is good for) and the **limitations** of the tool (i.e. its drawbacks or disadvantages). The features of language that are used in any particular context are very much connected with what that communication tool can or cannot do, and the different purposes we use it for.

*Activity*

List some new communication tools, for example:

*   txting (SMS);
*   computer-based email;
*   blogs;
*   chatrooms (e.g. msn, IM);
*   social networking sites;
*   other kinds of websites (e.g. for specialist interests, commercial sites, media sources, encyclopedias, etc.).

Then list the constraints – that is, the affordances and limitations – associated with each of the communication tools on the list.

To get you started, here are some constraints of mobile phone txting (SMS), which you can add to:

*Affordances*:

> cheap;
> editable;
> mobile (can txt anytime, anywhere).

*Limitations*:

> limited number of characters;
> can accidentally send a message to the wrong person;
> if plans rely on being able to txt, difficult if phone goes wrong.

You may find that the same quality or characteristic can feature as both a possible affordance and limitation: for example, the factor of mobility, above, is good because it allows people to make arrangements 'on the hoof'; but then, if for some reason the phone system fails, individuals can be left stranded.

(There is a commentary on this activity in the back of the book.)

## Global communication?

We are often told that our new communication technologies have allowed us to communicate 'globally'; and it is certainly true that systems such as email, instant messaging or social networking sites can put us in touch with people on the other side of the planet. But the ability to reach across vast distances should not lead us to think that new technologies have automatically bridged cultural gaps, as a result.

The writers of this book are from the UK and the USA, and our focus is largely on the language and cultural shifts that are taking place within an Anglo-American context.

But these trends and cultural shifts are not the same everywhere. Different countries and different cultures have adopted new technologies in very different ways.

For example, in Sweden, the most popular social networking site for 12–15 year olds is Bilddagboken (Picture Diary), where photos can be uploaded (Findahl, 2009). However, in the Netherlands, the social networking site Hyves is the preferred choice and the fourth most visited website in the country (www.alexa.com/siteinfo/hyves.nl). In Japan, Mixi.jp is the most popular social networking site, ranking as the tenth most visited website (www.alexa.com/topsites/countries/JP), while in the UK, Facebook features as the second most visited site (www.alexa.com/topsites/countries/GB).

These figures suggest that social networking online has been embraced more in the UK than in Japan.

Mobile phones have also been adopted differently across the world. In the Western world, history tells us that everyone once had landlines and then gradually embraced mobile phones, with many now giving up their unused landlines. In Europe, there are now 11 per cent more mobile phones than people, suggesting that many even have more than one mobile phone. In Africa, the use of mobile phones has also been growing rapidly. Mobile phones have been embraced more and in place of land- lines. There are many in Africa who never had a landline and now have a mobile phone. In less than ten years, the number of people in Africa with a mobile phone has risen from 2 per cent to 28 per cent (Tryhorn, 2009).

Also, mobile phones are used differently around the world. While the trend has not taken off in the UK or USA, in Africa it is common to use mobile phones to pay for purchases and to use the phone for banking purposes, such as wire money transfers (Greenwood, 2009). Mobile internet was embraced much earlier in Japan than in the UK and mobile phones are also used for paying for things like public transport. And in the USA, the popularity of txting grew more slowly than in the UK.

These cultural differences are often related to a number of factors, including the fact that there are different infrastructures and different amounts of investment in the new technology. For example, the infra- structure for broadband internet and mobile phone towers requires more effort and investment in a country such as the USA, which is spread out, as opposed to the UK, where populations are more densely organised in cities. Also, countries like Sweden have a faster and more developed broadband system than the USA because of different attitudes towards government investment. In Sweden, the government subsidised the construction and gave tax breaks to encourage investment, and in Japan the government provided low-interest loans and paid for the development in rural areas (Hansell, 2009). Without such assistance, broadband still lags behind in the USA compared with many other countries – it is slower and many, particularly rural, areas lack coverage.

Cultural differences in how we use technology may also be related to broader cultural practices. Baron and af Segerstad (2010) examined how mobile phones are used in public spaces in Sweden, the USA and Japan. They found that many of the differences between how people from these different countries use mobile phones in public can be related back to broader cultural differences in how they view public space. For example, generally, people from Swedish and Japanese cultural groups tend to be quieter in public spaces than Americans. When applied to mobile phones, this meant that they found Americans to be more comfortable speaking more loudly in public spaces and talked more on mobile phones, whereas Swedish and Japanese participants were more likely to txt. This also might explain why txting took longer to become popular in the USA. However, people from all three countries said they disapproved of those who spoke loudly on phones in public, Japanese participants expressing the strongest disapproval. Of the three cultural groups, Swedish participants were most likely to talk on their phone at a cash register and to use their mobile phone while eating with others.

Scollon (2001) saw a distinctive difference in mobile phone 'etiquette' between people in Finland and in Hong Kong, while working in both those countries. He claimed that, while Finns have one of the largest per capita ownership rates of mobile phones, their use is comparatively limited, and having one's phone switched off is not considered rude. In contrast, in Hong Kong there is an expectation that one's phone should always be on, and that, if someone has their phone turned off, this is seen as a problem.

Studies such as those described above are very interesting, but considerable caution is necessary to avoid seeing the behaviours described as characteristic of all group members, or as true for all time. Mobile phone norms of behaviour are likely to vary considerably according to, for example, occupation and age; while, even in the space of a few years, new conventions can become established. Think, for example, how there are now 'quiet' coaches on trains in the UK where phone calls are not allowed. As each new communication technology arrives, new rules for public behaviour have to be negotiated to accommodate it.

## Extension activities

1    In a special edition of *The Times* devoted to new communication technologies, journalists tested out what instructions for activities could be successfully communicated by txt. The special edition was triggered by the fact that a surgeon in the Congo, Africa, had conducted a life-saving amputation on a young man by getting txted instructions from an expert in London. Because of the extent of mobile phone coverage in the Congo, txting was the most reliable form of communication.

Adopting a more light-hearted approach, the journalists txted each other on how to change a car tyre; how to make a soufflé; and how to put make-up on.

Choose some activities and write some txt message instructions on how to go about them – for example, preparing a drink, building something, writing an assignment. How successfully can you communicate instructional meanings?

If you have a free choice of information sources, how do you normally get instructions for doing something you need to learn about?

2    With a partner, consider what you think are the norms for mobile phone behaviour in the UK. What is considered acceptable? And what is considered rude?

If you have had the chance to experience mobile phone use in a different culture, what were the norms for that particular group? How was it different from the UK?

3    Explore the Dutch SNS, Hyves (www.hyves.nl) and/or Skyrock (www. skyrock.com), which is popular in France. How do these sites encourage social interaction online? Why do you think they are popular in other countries but not in the UK?

4    Choose a country to research and produce a report on technology habits in that country. Here are some links for gathering data:

- Alexa: www.alexa.com/topsites/countries
- World Internet Project: www.worldinternetproject.net/
- Pew Internet and American Life Project: www.pewinternet.org/.
- And if you are interested in more detail regarding use in the United Kingdom: Oxford Internet Survey: http://microsites.oii.ox.ac.uk/oxis/.

three

# e-language 1: txting; email; discussion forums

## Aims of this unit

- To explore the features of language associated with the genres above.
- To explore the functions of language associated with the genres above.

## The language of txting

### LANGUAGE FEATURES

Although there are certain language strategies that many txters share, individuals will have their own linguistic **repertoires** of styles. In the same way, the common category of 'clothes' is shared by us all, but is subject to extreme individual variety. An individual's **idiolect** is as apparent in the world of txting as in any other language environment. Indeed, **forensic linguistics** has shown this rather dramatically, where a murderer, Peter Chapman, tried to give himself an alibi by txting on the phone of his murder victim (Forensic Linguistics Institute, 2010). But forensics showed that the txting style he'd adopted did not match the style of the victim.

Individuals don't have just one style of language in any environment, though, in the same way that they don't just have one outfit in their wardrobe. They have a repertoire, or range of styles, to suit different contexts. What follows, then, is an exploration of some broad features txters might have in common, while recognising that there will be some important variations between them.

A study conducted in 2003 (Thurlow, 2003) of university students' txt messages asked them to contribute some recent messages they had sent on their mobile phones to a corpus of language use. When analysed for distinctive features of language, the following common patterns were found:

- shortenings (missing end letters), e.g. 'lang' for 'language';
- contractions (missing middle letters), e.g. 'gd' for 'good';
- 'g' clipping (final letter missing), e.g. 'goin'' for 'going';
- other clippings, e.g. 'hav' for 'have';
- acronyms and initialisms, e.g. 'v' for 'very';
- letter/number homophones, e.g. '1' for 'one';
- non-conventional spellings, e.g. 'sum' for 'some';
- accent stylisation (speaker tries to represent a particular pronunciation, for example regional speech), e.g. 'wivout' for 'without';
- non-alphabetic symbols;
- emoticons.

In the corpus of 544 messages, the average message length was 14 'words' (including single symbols) and 65 characters. Given that, at the time, the maximum message length allowed was 160 characters, Thurlow concludes that txters were being what he called **dialogic** – that is, batting messages backwards and forwards in quite rapid sequences. It seemed that, with generous free txt allowances, people felt able to send several short messages and be more interactive, rather than piling all their information into a single package. This kind of **interactivity** is very conversation-like and is one of the reasons why people often describe SMS as a **hybrid**, or mixture: it can be interactive like speech, while being written using keyboard strokes.

Thurlow proposes a number of **sociolinguistic maxims**, or triggering factors, to explain some of the features above. These are:

- speed – txters have to speed up their pace of communication, so need to take short cuts;
- brevity – txters have only a limited space for their communication, so need to omit any elements that are not strictly necessary for understanding;

- **paralinguistic** restitution – txters need to find ways to replace the aspects of physical communication (such as body language) that are absent;
- **phonological** approximation – txters want to build in ways for their readers to 'hear' their voice, so try to change the written language to represent this.

*Activity*

In order to explore the idea of interactivity and also consider the range of features and maxims listed above, read through the txt exchange below (Text 3:1). This exchange is between two women, Denise and Laura, who are work colleagues and friends living in the north of England. They planned to meet on the evening in question and had suggested a pub in town. Denise starts the exchange by asking for a reminder about the pub's location.

Denise's txts are italicised and Laura's are in regular type. Line numbers refer to each person's complete message sent on each occasion:

1   How many of Thurlow's suggested features can you find in this data?
2   Are there further features that you would consider typical of this type of communication?
3   What explanations would you give for the occurrence of the language features you've identified?
4   To what extent do these participants each have their own individual style of composition?
5   Are there features here that you would use, or that are used by people you communicate with?

(Note: there is a commentary on this activity at the back of the book.)

23

## Text 3:1 Wher is pub?

| | |
|---|---|
| 1 | *wher is pub?* |
| 2 | Near minster on petergate |
| 3 | *Ah I remba – am drivin as up 2 nek in wrk. Do u want a lift?* |
| 4 | No am on my bike thanks ☺ |
| 5 | *On way need 2 get petrol 1st* |
| 6 | Okay |
| 7 | *Havin total nitemare jst put petrol in my deisal car! No idea hw lng wil b. Wil txt as soon as pos x* |
| 8 | oh flippin eck! Don't worry just get car sorted we can do another time xx |
| 9 | *Ok is complete piser* |
| 10 | Not kidding easily done tho |
| 11 | *Jst setin of 4hme – strangely traumatic! Wud u b up 4 anotha try nxt wk? V sory @ ths* |
| 12 | sure suggest some times |
| 13 | *Bak hme – am goin 2 put sticka on fuel cap! Wil cst me @ £100! If hd turnd car on wudve blown up engine – hpe u nt 2 pisd off wiv me. Can do nxt wed or th* |
| 14 | *urs – wil buy dina x* |
| 15 | Thurs would be good |

## LANGUAGE FUNCTIONS

As well as the features involved in this new form of communication, a language-focused approach also looks at the range of functions that txts are used for. As part of his research, Thurlow (2003) classified the different txts that he collected according to a range of possible functions. The headings below have been adapted from his research. The examples given are from 60 undergraduate students reporting their last six txt messages on their phones at a single point in 2007. This data was collected specifically for this book.

(Note that the examples below, on pp. 25–7 occurred separately, on different individuals' phones: in other words, they are not sequential exchanges.)

1    Look at the various functions listed in Text 3:2, and the explanations
     for each category. Does this list cover all that you use your phone for?
     If not, add further headings to this list.
2    Do any txts have more than one function, in this collection and in your
     experience?

(Note: there is no commentary on this activity.)

## Text 3:2 Txting functions

### Informational/practical function
This function is about asking for information or negotiating practical
issues.

Examples:

*   cud u do me favor, al hasnt got internet. CUd ya luk wot time
    trains are frm headingley round 5ish plz x x x
*   where is good to eat in didsburyish? love G
*   What is name of australia womens footie team
*   Am going to try and sell the computer workstation b4 i do r u
    sure u dont want it or ny of yr friends want it xx
*   Hey! sorry forgot the milk, remember to get it pretty please, make
    sure its organic! love katxx

### Social planning function
This function is about planning social activities.

Examples:

*   You still gonna come to pub? Not at work today so if you wanna
    make it earlier?
*   U eat yet? Wana get food?
*   Cn we go end ov oct wen I get payed
*   Hey everyone quick reminder. Party at mine Tues for my and
    Gina's birthday!

*continued . . .*

Text 3:2
Txting
functions
continued . . .

- PAM! ONE NIGHT ONLY ARE FILMING THEIR VIDEO NEXT WED AND WANT PEOPLE TO BE IN IT!!! Fancy giving it a go? xxx

## Friendship maintenance function

This function is about keeping in touch with people, and showing interest in them and concern about them.

Examples:

- Hope u have a better day today. Ring me if u need anything x
- Omg!!! U leg-end! See i told you you would :-D HOORAH! *biiig hug* xxx
- Sitting here watching sex and the city thinking of old times. Hope you are well and hope to see you again soon X
- Hi Sophie x Hope u r settling in OK Hows things? x x
- I love how tonga are all 8 foot tall built like brick shit houses, wearing kits with tribal designs on. England on the other hand are short, pale, neatly turned out toffs wearing skin tight shirts that look like they were designed for jockeys

## Phatic/salutation function

This is like a linguistic 'prod' – a brief message to remind someone that you are there.

Examples:

- Good morning! I've just woken up! Xxx
- Howdy partner!
- Hey up!
- Psst!
- BOO!!!!!!!!

## Romantic/sexual function

This is as it sounds – expressing romantic emotion and sexual interest.

Examples:
- Hey sexi, gd luk @ football hope ya win see ya 2night xxxxxxxxxxxxxxxxx
- I love you lots xxxxx
- Na nite *cuddle* mwah x x x x x

*continued . . .*

Text 3:2
Txting
functions
continued . . .

- Aww baby u make me smile ☺ x x x
- I miss youuuuuu ☹ lovelove xXxXx

## Chain/corporate/advertising function

This function relates to the commercial base of txting – the fact that it is communication that is bought and sold.

Chain messages try to get you to send more txts; corporate mails are from organisations who are using txting as a way to reach their audience; advertising via txt is very cheap compared, say, with a magazine or TV advert.

Examples:

- this is a txt to say that you are a very special friend to me and you have made a difference in my life. send this to all your friends whether you see them all the time or havent seen them for ages . . . just to show you care. if you send this within 5 minutes to 5 friends . . . good luck will come your way. if you dont, then something bad will happen 2moro.
- This is a toast to all us beautiful ladies for 2007! For the men who r fortunate enough to have us, the losers who had us and lost us and the very lucky bastards who r still yet 2 meet us! Send this to all the beautiful women u know! Don't break the chain! x x
- It's National Good Looking Day! Send this to someone gorgeous. But don't send it back to me. I've been getting this f**king message all day!
- O2 Extras: FREE 24-7 Footie clips every Monday in September
- Thanks for your entry. We hope you are a winner. Good luck!

*Activity*

Now repeat the collecting exercise described earlier: each group member should contribute six txts from their phone, preferably those sent previously by group members themselves rather than those received (sent previously means before reading this book; txts sent by group members themselves will not need further permissions to be sought). Remember only to contribute those txts that you are happy for others to see.

Decide which are the most appropriate functional headings for your txts.

When your data collection is complete, analyse it for either language features, or functions, or both. Pursue your own questions about the data, but here are some starting points for you to consider:

- How much abbreviation is in evidence in your data, compared with standardised writing? Txting habits might have changed as predictive txt has developed, and as some phones have regular keyboards instead of phone keys.
- How many of your txts involved images, or other kinds of file transfers? As phones have developed camera (and video) functions, it may be that txts are often accompanied by other kinds of messages.
- Are some functions more frequently employed than others? If so, why do you think that's so?
- To what extent are messages multi-functional (i.e. fulfilling more than one purpose simultaneously)?
- To what extent is it difficult to understand the messages in your collection? Is this because txting is essentially a private form of communication where txters have their own shared meanings?

(Note: there is a commentary on this activity at the back of the book. Obviously the actual examples will not be predictable, but the commentary will offer some information on likely patterns found in the collection.)

## The language of email

As there is no one language of txting but rather some broadly shared conventions, so email can be seen as a genre of communication, but one where there is considerable variation according to audience, purpose and other aspects of context (for example, the communication tool being used, as email can be written not only on computers but also on Smartphones such as Blackberrys).

Rather than starting with linguistic features this time, the initial focus is on email functions.

*Txt or email?*

What makes you choose one of these forms of communication over the other? Are they good for very different purposes? To help you think about this, read the account below:

> On Monday, April 16, 2007, on the campus of Virginia Tech in Blacksburg, Virginia, USA, a student called Seung-Hui Cho went on a shooting spree. In two separate attacks, approximately two hours apart, Cho killed 32 people and wounded many others before committing suicide.
>
> Once the incident was over, the course of events was reviewed to assess the effectiveness of the university's response. One criticism levelled at the university was that they had been slow to tell students to stay off campus: they had used email, which students did not check regularly, rather than SMS to students' phones, which would have been quicker and more effective.

Do you agree with this analysis? In the event of a crisis, how would you spread information most quickly to your fellow students? Are there other, happier, situations where one or other of these forms of communication is a better option? Or are there further forms of communication that would be better than either txting or email?

(Note: there is no commentary on this activity.)

*What's in your email inbox?*

How many different kinds of email do you send and receive?
    Below is a possible list of email functions. Do your mails fit under these headings easily, or are there some that need further headings?
    Are there some mails in your inbox that are multi-purpose?

- Interpersonal – e.g. mails between friends.
- Organisational – e.g. mails to and from an organisation that the individual belongs to, for example a workplace or educational establishment.
- Social/leisure – e.g. mails about hobbies or special interest groups.

**29**

- Service sector – e.g. mails to do with bookings, online orders, etc.
- Advertising – e.g. promotional material, information about offers, etc.
- Cybercrime – e.g. **'phishing'** emails trying to get an individual's personal details such as bank account numbers, etc.

(Note: there is no commentary on this activity.)

## THE LANGUAGE OF EMAIL STYLES

In the previous activity, you will have seen that emails come in many different shapes and sizes. Because of this, it's impossible to say 'this is the language of email'. What you will have seen is a wide range of **stylistic** choices, probably ranging from informal language features in your emails between friends, and more formal choices in any you've received from organisations, such as from the managers of your educational or work establishment. In general, the wider the audience for communication, the more formal and careful the style is likely to be, as people tend to err on the safe side of politeness where they can't assume shared understanding. However, there are exceptions. For example, advertisements may assume an informal style because they are simulating a friendship with you. Similarly, a phishing email, which tries to discover your personal details in order to steal from you, may choose an informal style in order to catch you off guard; but equally, this type of mail can also be formal if it imitates organisational communication.

As will be clear from the explanation above, you are likely to encounter as many different styles in email as you might see in writing and receiving traditional, paper-based letters. However, as with traditional letters, there are some aspects of email language that you can say with some certainty are likely to feature. For example, think about:

- the machine code that comes with the email – date and time stamps, the email address of the sender;
- the details about recipients – who else, if any, has been included in the circulation;
- additions that an individual has set up to be automatic, such as a signature, role description, or links to websites;
- opening and closing routines;
- the subject line.

Although these aspects are likely to be present, how we interpret them is by no means a straightforward matter. For they are not simply factual aspects – each item of information carries social significance, for example:

- *Date and time*: you might interpret an email message differently if it was sent on a certain day (before or after you saw the writer) or at a certain time (first thing in the morning compared with late at night).
- *Email address*: a writer's email address tells you something either about their personal naming choices, their group membership, or their organisational affiliation; if they have more than one address that they use, their choice of one or another will tell you something about which identity they are assuming on any one occasion.
- *Recipients*: you might feel differently about a message if it's being sent to a large group of people, as opposed to just yourself.
- *Signatures*: how an individual describes themselves in their automatic signature tells you about how they want to be seen (or how their organisation wants them to appear).
- *Openings and closings*: the nature of the greetings and farewell tokens used says much about the relationship between the participants in the email exchange.
- *The subject line*: this has to attract the attention of the inbox owner enough to open it, and express something in a kind of shorthand about the nature of the contents.

*Activity*

Read the email exchange in Text 3:3.
 You won't be able to discuss the email addresses and signatures, as these have been removed for purposes of anonymity. However, there is much to say about the nature of this exchange, as evidenced by the participants' language choices and by some of the other elements that are present in the data:

1    How would you describe the relationship between the participants and the way this exchange develops as it goes along? Give linguistic evidence for your interpretation. (The exchange reads from the bottom up; CAB refers to 'Citizens Advice Bureau'.)
2    Are there elements of these messages that you experience as frequent aspects of email communication in general?

(Note: there is a commentary on this activity at the back of the book.)

## Text 3:3 Email exchange

From: [details omitted]
Date: 24 September 2004 10:21 a.m.
To: [details omitted]
Subject: Re: Reference

Oh linguist! Guy is no longer gender specific - try watching Friends etc. Guys and Gals is an old musical. Although Dorothy was in The Wizard of Oz.

-------------------------------------------------------------------------------------------

From: [details omitted]
To: [details omitted]
Sent: Friday, September 24, 2004 10:15 a.m.
Subject: Re: Reference

Typical man assuming the accountant is a male tut tut!!!! I'm sure Dorothy with be delighted to meet you though! Rosie

-------------------------------------------------------------------------------------------

From: [details omitted]
Date: 24 September 2004 8:10 a.m.
To: [details omitted]
Subject: Re: Reference

Thanks. New finance guy sounds good.

Nick

-------------------------------------------------------------------------------------------

From: [details omitted]
To: [details omitted]
Sent: Thursday, September 23, 2004 6:24 p.m.
Subject: Re: Reference

sorry Nick been away and off for a while will get it posted tomorrow it is already written. Good luck with it, Rosie

P.s. we have someone for the finance post at last a very nice accountant from bishopthorpe.

-------------------------------------------------------------------------------------------

From: [details omitted]
Date: 22 September 2004 7:14 a.m.
To: [details omitted]
Subject: Reference

Hi Rosie

Any chance of you sending that reference to CAB? They were enquiring about it when I saw them yesterday.

Regards
Nick

The email exchange you have been studying in Text 3:3 consists of a fairly simple **chain** format, where messages in their entirety are batted back and forth. However, this is not the only structure that email participants produce, for electronic messages allow respondents to manipulate the messages being sent to them, and incorporate the reshaped originals into their replies. This potential for creative co-construction arises from the **non-linear**, **porous** nature of electronic texts, compared with their paper-based predecessors. Some examples of different strategies follow below.

The first email in Text 3:4 was sent from one business colleague to another. The second email is the reply. In replying, the respondent chose to divide up the original text, and reply to each section separately. Sometimes, writers of emails do this where they are replying to a number of different questions, or issues. Crystal (2001) calls this strategy **framing**. In this example, the writers know each other so well that the respondent doesn't feel the need to do a greeting or a full sign-off, but merely inserts lines in response to the different topics covered and questions asked.

## Text 3:4 Business exchange

*Original email*:

Subject: trainees

Hi Marge
Nice minutes - Stuart liked them alot! Hear nothing was resolved on the Leader issue - but would like to hear your version of this!
    I'm not sure if you know that Mike has additional trainees than indicated on that initial list - as you are dealing with them at the moment - they are on a list in your p/h. Sorry!
    Also I would like to check out some dates to see if you're around to feed my delightful cat - ie. US conference etc — but I am going to go home and work this afternoon before coming back in to meet up with the Intercultural group for the evening - so if you fancy a cuppa let me know as I will be going via Tesco's and intend to but some thing nice to eat, like cake!
speak soon
Lxx
[+automatic signature]

-----------------------------------------------------------------------------------

*continued . . .*

**Text 3:4**
**Business**
**exchange**
continued . . .

> ***Reply, using 'framing' technique (the respondent's replies are in italic type):***
>
> Subject: trainees
> Hi Marge
>
> Nice minutes - Stuart liked them alot! Hear nothing was resolved on the Leader issue - but would like to hear your version of this!
>
> *far too dangerous a topic for an email, dear . . . let's go for a pint!*
>
> I'm not sure if you know that Mike has additional trainees than indicated on that initial list - as you are dealing with them at the moment - they are on a list in your p/h. Sorry!
>
> *I forgive you*
>
> Also I would like to check out some dates to see if you're around to feed my delightful cat - ie. US conference etc — but I am going to go home and work this afternoon before coming back in to meet up with the Intercultural group for the evening - so if you fancy a cuppa let me know as I will be going via Tesco's and intend to but some thing nice to eat, like cake!
>
> > *cat yes probably, cake yes definitely xM*
>
> speak soon
> Lxx
> [+automatic signature]

It is possible to use the same type of strategy as shown in Text 3:4, but without breaking up the original email text. In fact, Condon and Cech (2004) suggest that, when we respond to emails that ask a number of different questions or raise different topics, we tend to cover these same issues in our replies in the order in which they occurred in the original. This is regardless of whether we break up the original text or just write a continuous response as a single text.

This activity involves thinking about to what extent writers might do as Condon and Cech suggest – mirror each other's email structure.

Read through the email exchange in Text 3:5, which is between two professional writers, Elin and Hannah, who are planning some joint work. Hannah is preparing to visit Elin, who lives in Sweden. Elin is bilingual in English and Swedish; Hannah speaks only English.

Work through the texts, deciding as you go what the themes are. Do this first for the original email from Elin (the first text), then look at how those themes have been responded to by Hannah. Basing your view on this data, to what extent are Condon and Cech right in their proposal that we mirror the themes of the emails sent to us when we reply?

(There is a commentary on this activity at the back of the book.)

## Text 3:5 Preparing to visit

*Original email:*

Subject: next visit

Dear Hannah,

Hope all is well with you. Time flies!

About 8 degrees and rain at the moment. Hopefully that will have changed by the time you get here next week.

I do not have anything scheduled in [place omitted] next week, but perhaps it would be a good idea to get together and brainstorm some ideas for the article, and/or possible discuss more ideas for the fall?

I am busy in [place omitted] on Thursday and Friday but would be happy to go to [place omitted] on any of the other days. Or, if you are planning a visit to [place omitted] we could meet here for lunch on any of the days? Mostly reading proofs right now.

Let me know if you'll be to busy so that you would rather communicate by email (lots of negative politeness strategies here . . . :-))

cheers,
Elin

----------------------------------------------------------------------

*continued . . .*

**Text 3:5**
**Preparing to**
**visit**

continued . . .

> *Reply:*
>
> hi Elin,
> yes very cold here too *sigh*
> good idea to get together - i'm not likely to be in [place omitted] this
> time but don't have anything planned for Tuesday, so we could meet
> then in [place omitted] if you were happy to come over?
> let's plan something for the journal, great idea.
> if i get a minute maybe i could make some suggestions? happy to be
> overruled tho'. . .
> cheers,
> Hannah

So far, the focus has been on the different overall textual structures that might present themselves in email data – first a simple chained exchange, then responses that either chunked the original text into separate, more manageable, sections, or else mirrored the order of the original's themes, in constructing a reply.

Regardless of the textual shape chosen, however, what should be apparent is that email exchanges often involve negotiations of **identity**, because each time a person writes a message, they are putting forward a certain view of themselves and are making assumptions about their interlocutor. Whatever the message content, writers don't just pass on information; they show an attitude towards what they are writing about and towards their intended reader(s). In short, wherever and whenever human beings are interactive, interpersonal strategies oil the wheels of action.

From the earliest days of email usage, researchers have reported on the emotional nature of some email communication, coining the term **flaming** to describe the way in which writers can appear to lose control of their emotions in electronic environments (the idea of flaming has also been associated with all the other types of computer-based communication). According to Turnage (2007), there are specific aspects of language associated with the perception of an email as potentially abusive, including the use of swear words, writing totally in capitals, and excessive amounts of exclamation or question marks. However, while the phenomenon of flaming is certainly evidence that electronic **discourse** can arouse emotion, it is difficult to single out particular language features and simply say that they are offensive, for meaning depends very much on context and the relationship between the individuals concerned.

A more individually focussed approach for considering writers' choice of style comes from Communication Accommodation Theory (CAT) (Giles and St Clair, 1979). Applied originally to accent features in speech, this theory focuses on the choice of style as an individual's attempt to move towards (converge with) or move away from (diverge from) another in terms of social distance. This theory would suggest that those who want to align with others are likely to try to match their interlocutor's choices, while those who want to maximise their social distance will make markedly different stylistic choices.

## *Activity*

The email exchange in Text 3:6 is between an events manager (Carrie) and a colleague responsible for supporting the use of technology in presentations (Patrick). Carrie used a presentation area some time ago and discovered that an important technical tool (which she terms 'the magic pen') has disappeared.

Analyse the language choices made by these communicators. To what extent does Patrick mirror Carrie's choices, and what does that tell us about their relationship?

In strictly functional terms, Carrie's email is a form of complaint. Does it come across as this? If not, what else is going on in this communication?

(Note: there is a commentary on this activity at the back of the book.)

## **Text 3:6 The magic pen**

Subject: the magic pen

hi Patrick,
last time I was in presentation b it was unusable because some daft bugger has walked off with the pen. I know you mailed us all about this, but if nobody 'fesses up is there any chance of getting a replacement?
Carrie
[+automatic signature]

-----------------------------------------------------------------------------------------

*continued . . .*

**Text 3:6 The magic pen** continued . . .

---

Subject: the magic pen

Carrie
Where HAVE you been!
I replaced the "pen" Monday 22nd October after the felony was discovered and the offender chose not to return it despite the "Pen Amnesty".

I have now tethered both pens to the lectern (using industrial strength cable) as these pens cost £75 each and I pay for them out of my own pocket.

No doubt the next thing will be some herbert trying to make his/her way out of the building dragging a beech effect chipboard lectern from his braces!
Thanks for your interest.

See You
Patrick
[+automatic signature]

PS (disclaimer).The above comments are merely a personal observation and should not be taken as representative views of the [organisation name omitted] :-)

---

## The language of discussion forums

Discussion forums, also known as bulletin boards, are **asynchronous**, like email, but different from email in being much more open, public spaces. The idea of audience is therefore very different, with people able to predict much less confidently who might be reading their **posts**.

Forums tend to be interest-based, with a forum available for just about every kind of special interest, from dog breeding to tattoos and from knitting and crochet to astronomy. The assumption, then, is that, although one's posts might be read by complete strangers, they are likely to have at least one interest in common.

Beyond forums that are theme-based, a forum-type tool is also found attached to many media websites, for example those of newspapers, radio stations or TV channels. So it is now common for written articles or oral comments made by journalists to appear in an online version, then to be responded to by members of the public who log on and want to reply.

The forum tool has therefore turned many erstwhile monologues into dialogues, sometimes involving many people.

Because discussion forums are so open, they are sometimes run by a moderator whose role is to monitor the language use that's employed by participants in order to avoid offence. However, many are also self-regulated, relying on the community itself to police its own output. When someone joins a forum community, it is common practice to have to agree to some general rules of behaviour. This tends to focus on language, for obvious reasons.

Because discussion forums are about what they say – discussion – an obvious focus in researching their language use is to look at how discussion works in this kind of environment. Questions that might be asked (not in any particular order), include:

- In a multi-party context, how do people make it clear who they are responding to?
- How do people manage agreements and disagreements?
- How do people initiate new topics?
- Do some posts get much longer or more frequent responses than others and, if so, why?
- What are some of the different functions of the posts – for example, are some more information-seeking/giving while others are more persuasive?
- How do people present themselves in their names and any profile details?
- Are there particular styles of writing and presentation that are noticeable?
- Do participants presume much common ground in terms of shared knowledge and values?
- Do people use links and connections to other sites to support their views?
- What would you say were the major concerns and topics of interest for the group you are studying?

### Activity

Text 3:7 is an extract from an online forum where people can post classified ads offering small items for sale.

Read the posts and analyse how the participants negotiate for the sale of the item. (Note: A, B, C, D and E are all different individuals.)

(Note: there is a commentary on this activity at the back of the book.)

## Text 3:7 Items for sale

Forums > General: Classifieds, For Sale > 19'' CRT iiyama visionmaster pro 450

**A:**   19'' CRT iiyama visionmaster pro 450 I have the above monitor for sale.
As new, unboxed but with all cables & instructions.
Collect from central London. It's large and very heavy.
Only £10! No offers.

**B:**   Damn, I would only going to offer £9.50 for it.
Oh well.

**A:**   Shame. For an extra 50p it could have been yours and you could have carried it back.

**C:**   is it 1 of these?
http://www.ciao.co.uk/iiyama_Vision_Master_Pro_450__18911
I could do with a new monitor . . . how heavy??

**A:**   That's the one.
How heavy? Umm . . . "very"?
According to the booklet, "net weight = 28Kg"

**C:**   its very tempting
although i do drive . . . i've become lazy with a 6 zone travel card . .

**D:**   Ooh, Ooh!
If I took a taxi would that work?

**C:**   £10.50

**D:**   £11.00. aw, my lowly 15'' flatscreen is so bad I can't see shades of colours any more!

**C:**   I work in Soho . . . could stagger home with it
Once on the underground then its Liverpool st . . . and a short walk home once i get off the train
I've done nothing today . . could have picked it up today

**D:**   I'm not working at the moment (new job starts in a few weeks) so I could be there any time. Though I live on the 3rd floor, no lift so I'd take it one floor and then take a rest!
Taxi cab door to door!
(It would seem like the lack of response from A means he is negotiating with someone, doh!)

**A:**   Nope, just that I'm doing other stuff. This is a forum, not an MSN chat :-)
The monitor is fantastic, and cost over £300 new (albeit that was a few years ago). I don't have a desktop PC any more, so don't need the monitor.

*continued . . .*

**Text 3:7 Items for sale** continued . . .

> Compared to an LCD the quality of the picture is fantastic. Very high resolu-
> tion, very bright, very clear. Compared to an LCD it's also very big. That's the
> downside.
> I don't mind whether you come by taxi, on foot, or by elephant. I live near
> Russell Square and you'd need to collect.
> Fight amongst yourselves and whoever offers the most - it's yours!
> If there were two of you, it'd be easy to carry from doorstep up to a flat.
> Otherwise, a trolley (or something with wheels) would really help.
>
> **D:**  It was merely a joke A my dear, fun and entertaining speculation.
> **E:**  I have one for free D, and since you're only 5 mins from me, I'd deliver and
> carry it up the stairs for you!
> Then C can have A's and no fighting need ensue!
> **D:**  I'M IN LOVE!! But I think E already knew that!
> **E:**  Tis yours then!
> **A:**  As it seems one of the bidders has dropped out (I can't compete with free plus
> free delivery!) it's yours, C, for a tenner.
> **D:**  Thank you A for posting this thread even though I now bow to Monsieur C
> I wouldn't have the promise of a new monitor were it not for you!
> **A:**  haha - two happy people, and only £10 involved :)

*Activity*

The data in Text 3:8 is from a different kind of forum context. This is an
international student forum, where university students from different countries
meet to discuss their views on particular topics related to language and culture.
The data shows an initial post by Syeda, then the exchanges that ensue
between Syeda and two different respondents, Andrea (in the UK) and Susan
(in the USA).

   This time, focus on why the exchanges are sustained or not, in the two
cases. What language strategies are used, with the effect of either prolonging
or shutting down the discussion?

(Note: there is no commentary on this activity.)

# Text 3:8 International student forum

*Syeda and Andrea*:

Hello Everyone,
My name is Syeda and Im Zambian but I am currently studying in Sweden at [university name omitted] as an exchange student from Namibia.
I am studying Sociology and Intercultural studies and in the future I want to become a psychiatrist because my major is psychology back home.

Syeda

Would you specialise in anything? There are so many specific fields within psychology!

Andrea xxx

Hi Andrea,
I want to specialise in industrial or forensic pychology.At the momemt I can only do industrial psychology because the university im at doesnt offer forensic pychology so I have put that on hold.

Can you explain what you mean by industrial psychology, I've never heard of it before.

Andrea xxx

Hi Andrea,
Industrial psychology deals with group dynamics and if I graduate I can work in the human resource department in companies like banks or other institutions and will have to assess the workers performance and find ways of motivating them among other things.Mostly it has to do with human resource.
If you have any oter questions pls feel free to ask.I will decide anyway because I can choose to do clinical or counselling pyschology as well.Since I have been studying it for a year only I will decide which field suites me best because we will have a selection process at the end of the year as well as exams to determine who goes where.
Take care.

It's not really the same but I am doing a module in Second Language Acquisition and TESOL and we did a bit about motivation and the factors that lead to how well a person learns another language. I was really interested in the different types of motivation and how these can be exploited to get the best of someone.

*continued . . .*

**Text 3:8 International student forum** continued . . .

When I was applying to uiversity psychology was the most popular degree course, that and law. Is it as popular in America and Sweden?

Andrea xxx

Hi I think it is popular in America but not too popular in Sweden most people opt for computer science degrees because they more marketable.I asked a swedish friend and she said most people prefer computer based courses.my flat mate is actually from england from rochdale.

**Syeda and Susan:**

Hello Everyone,
My name is Syeda and Im Zambian but I am currently studying in Sweden at [university name omitted] as an exchange student from Namibia.
I am studying Sociology and Intercultural studies and in the future I want to become a psychiatrist because my major is psychology back home.

Syeda

Psychology fascinates me - people fascinate me! I have taken five or six psych classes at [university name omitted]. Where would you like to practice psychology?

Welcome to the group.

Susan

Hi Susan,
Hope you are ok.I would like to practice psychology back home but I dont mind practicing it anywhere as long as I gain experience and find a suitable environment.

# Extension activities

This unit has focussed strongly on data, and you should therefore be in a good position to apply some of the analytical approaches you have tried here to data of your own. E-language is not hard to find, as electronic communication has become a regular experience for many people. Pieces of communication probably arrive in your various inboxes on a daily basis. However, you do need to think about the ethics of any research plans you develop.

Where you collect pieces of communication from individuals, particularly where the community in question is in a closed environment (for example, a password-protected forum), you need to seek permission from the participants to use their material. Where there is a very public and open site (for example, a 'Have Your Say' section of an online newspaper), it's clear that the participants were happy to broadcast their communication to the widest possible audience, so getting permission is not such an issue. Regardless of the nature of your material, no individual's name or personal details should be revealed in any way that makes them traceable.

# e-language 2:
# real-time writing;
# social networking sites

## Aims of this unit

- To explore the nature of synchronous writing.
- To explore the language environment of social networking sites.

## Real-time writing

Real-time writing, also called **synchronous** writing, or **interactive** writing, relies on participants being logged in and working at their screens at the same time. Usage of this kind of tool in the early days of the internet tended to involve communication (often with strangers) in large public chatrooms, but, as computers have become more embedded in our everyday existence, we have also been able to go online with people we know, in private spaces where we are able to decide who gets invited into our communities (for example, in social networking sites, or via instant message tools such as msn). And although chatrooms are often given bad publicity in the press (see Unit 7), there are many serious uses for real-time writing, including staff meetings, academic tutorials, and getting important information or help and support.

Interactive writing makes very different demands on participants compared with asynchronous communication such as email or discussion forums. For a start, real-time writing is composed on the hoof, like speech, so there is very little time for drafting and editing (although there is some, as elements can be deleted before the message is sent to the screen). In order to keep up with the speed of interaction, participants need to be able to compose at speed and to abbreviate, so this environment might well generate the same kinds of shortcuts seen in the other forms of communication studied so far.

However, one of the biggest differences between a tool such as SMS, and real-time writing, is that 'chat' participants might well find themselves in a multi-party interaction, as opposed to an exchange with a single individual. There are therefore problems of working out who any particular post to the screen is aimed at. This is made more complex by the fact that, depending on participants' composition speed, posts to the screen may or may not end up on the screen in the place where the writer intended. One early commentator (Werry, 1996) described the kind of text produced in chatrooms as a play where the characters' lines have all been jumbled up.

When looking at a **chatlog**, what you are seeing is a record of the result of the conversation – not the thing itself. There is an important difference, because of what was said above: the participants may have intended to place their response next to a particular line, but someone else got there first. In other words, the **seriality** of chatlog lines is no indication of **adjacency** relationships: or, put more simply, just because one line occurs after another does not mean it is a response to it.

Text 4:1 is an example of where a participant, Lucy, recognises that her line 'you liar' had ended up in the wrong place on the screen. Ryan is pretending that he is in the USA, when in fact he is in a building on the campus of a UK university, and Lucy's 'you liar' challenges this. Ryan retracts his statement by saying 'i mean jeffry manton' (this is the name of a university building). Lucy is bothered by her line being in the wrong place, because it looks as though she's saying 'you liar' in response to Ryan's being in the 'jeffry manton' building. She then writes an explanation of where she originally intended her line to go.

## Text 4:1 'You liar'

**Dawn**>>Ryan where are you channeling us from mate???
**Ryan**>>im in los angeles
**Carrie**>>does anyone know where Natalie is?
**Ryan**>>i mean jeffry manton
**Lucy**>>you liar
**Gregory**>>Lucky Bugger
**Ryan**>>yes
**Dawn**>>Which Natalie??
**Lucy**>>why are you in jeffry manton. (my "liar" bit was meant to come
in after "los angeles".)

Aside from issues of seriality and adjacency, what should be clear from the above example is that multi-party written dialogue can require participants to juggle many topics at once. Even in the short extract above, there is more than one conversation going on: topics include Ryan's whereabouts, Natalie's whereabouts and identity, and discourse management (i.e. Lucy's **metalanguage**). In addition, participants have to decide whether others are being playful or not, as in a virtual environment no one can really tell where others are physically located.

If many conversations are going on simultaneously, the question of who is addressing whom in their questions and comments can be problematic. In face-to-face dialogue, this is often easy to determine via interlocutors' eye gaze and physical proximity; but where such signals are absent, other strategies are needed. Werry (1996) suggests that participants in real-time writing contexts often have to pay extra attention to **addressivity** (i.e. strategies for naming) in order to regulate **turntaking** in a virtual environment. The extract in Text 4:2 shows addressivity in action: Lucy is managing two conversations at once, with Rachael and Anna. She distinguishes who she is addressing in each case by using the first names of the others in the room. Note that this sometimes results in some odd wordings – for example, in Lucy's final line.

## Text 4:2 Addressivity in action

> **Rachael**>>Well Hello there. My name is Rachael and I live in a small coastal villiage called Solva in south Wales but you're more likely to have heard of St.Davids which is where I went to school (3 miles from home).
> **Anna**>>I come from a little city in North Wales called Bangor. I'ts approximatly 90 mins drive from here
> **Lucy**>>What sort of accent would you said you had Rachael
> **Lucy**>>Oh your from Wales to Anna. Would you say that you had a strong Welsh accent?

Because **prosodic** aspects such as intonation are absent in written texts, writers have to work hard to represent the subtleties of meaning normally carried by the spoken voice. In writing, confusion can arise where in speech there would be no ambiguity. For example, in Text 4:3, the abbreviation 'btw' caused confusion because Andrew's 'by the way' sounded less like an explanation and more like a discourse marker at the start of an utterance. Simon clearly thinks it's the latter, because his 'what' signals that he is waiting for Andrew to finish. Notice, too, that 'god, andrew' (mild imprecation plus an address term), compared with 'god andrew' (**premodifier** plus address term), would have sounded very different in speech.

## Text 4:3 By the way

> **Sorcha**>>whats BTW
> **Andrew**>>By the way
> **Simon**>>what
> **Natalie**>>whats the hell is btw
> **Andrew**>>By the way, its computer jargon
> **Natalie**>>meaning
> **Dawn**>>Eh whats btw i am tres confused!!!
> **Sorcha**>>accordingly its too technical to understand
> **Natalie**>>try me
> **Sorcha**>>god andrew what have you started
> **Andrew**>>I'm no god, but thanks for the compliment

Where there is confusion, of course, there is also potential for play: perhaps Andrew deliberately exploited the confusion because he enjoyed the mayhem.

Below are three more chatlog extracts, called Texts 4:4, 4:5 and 4:6.

For each piece of data, comment on some of the aspects of real-time writing that are apparent in the data. You could consider areas such as:

- turntaking, seriality and adjacency;
- length of turns (Werry (1996) estimated that the average turn in his data was six words long);
- how far errors of spelling and other graphological aspects concern the participants;
- how aspects of voice are represented in writing;
- language play.

(There is a commentary on this activity at the back of the book.)

## Text 4:4 The connotations of colours

(Participants have been discussing the connotations of different colours.)

**Anna**>>I have always loved purple but I'm not quitesure why!
    Wht does a certain colour appeal to someone?
**Natalie**>>i love black.it's slimming
**Anna**>>I meant why !!
**Sorcha**>>shes just said why, cause its slimming
**Simon**>>and how is that useful to communication
**Rachael**>>I know what you mean, I love yellow! wonder what that says about me?
**Natalie**>>it communicates that your thinner than you actually are
**Anna**>>I was correcting myself 'cause I typed wht

## Text 4:5 How did you do that?

(In the chat tool being used, Ryan had logged into the chatroom but not logged out again. Lucy enters the room and clicks on his name, which is still on the screen, bringing him back into the room from his location on another part of the online site).

**Ryan**>>hi
**Lucy**>>hi Ryan
**Ryan**>>hello
**Lucy**>>how are you?
**Ryan**>>not bad
**Ryan**>>how did you do that
**Lucy**>>but not good?
**Lucy**>>do what?
**Ryan**>>talk to me
**Lucy**>>I am
**Ryan**>>no
**Lucy**>>what?
**Ryan**>>how did you talk to me i was not in a chat room
**Lucy**>>yeah you were. Your name was on the column at the side

## Text 4:6 Yehah

**Natalie**>>yeak
**Natalie**>>sorry yea
**Simon**>>why yeah
**Natalie**>>i dont mean it like yeah man i mean it like yeay
**Simon**>>what is the difference
**Natalie**>>it's happier and less cheesy
**Simon**>>and that is worthy of a yehah

## Social networking sites

**Social networking sites (SNSs)** combine many of the different communication tools we've looked at so far, within the same space. SNSs are web-based services that allow individuals to set up a profile for themselves and invite others to view their output. Participants can be made aware of the activity of others in their particular network.

Participants of SNSs can be highly interactive, communicating in real time via chat tools where others are online simultaneously, and leaving asynchronous posts on others' sites where they are not. SNSs really came into prominence with the rise of **Web 2.0** technologies, which allowed ordinary users to create their own web content, rather than being simply readers of pages with no opportunity to interact.

The names of particular sites come and go: at the time of writing, Facebook is a commonly used site, although there are growing objections to the fact that Facebook sells participants' data to advertisers.

SNSs such as Facebook create new unknown factors that affect how we present ourselves, and how others understand us. For a start, personal information about us is significantly more extensive than was the case in, for example, a phone book or other paper-based, linear directory. People can create profiles that incorporate images, video clips and sound files, making pages **multimodal** in their operation, and requiring multimodal communication skills in order to interpret them. Web 2.0 communication in general requires new kinds of literacy skills, involving the ability to move between different types of material from a wide range of sources, and to understand new kinds of connections – for example, those produced by **tagging**, a form of labelling that generates **semantic fields** from users' own associations.

Chandler (2006) sees individuals' web identities on sites such as Facebook as permanently 'under construction', as users constantly tinker with how they represent themselves online. He argues that creating a profile is akin to advertising oneself, and advertising to countless unknown others as well as those who are familiar from face-to-face encounters (the term 'friends' has a very loose connotation on SNSs, as many users have hundreds of 'friends' via a process of chain reaction). Although a user may therefore construct their own profile with certain ideas in mind, how the profile will be interpreted is beyond their control. For the analyst, however, the choices an individual has made for their profile are of course very revealing about the process of identity-construction.

The artful arrangement of elements to form a composite construction in art was long ago termed **bricolage** by the cultural theorist Levi Strauss. Chandler uses the bricolage idea to describe what individuals do when they create a homepage or SNS page for themselves, as they assemble a range of different elements to construct an identity. His 'Bricoleur's Web Kit', as set out below, both describes the process individuals might follow in doing this construction work, and provides a useful framework for an analyst to use. The Web Kit offers an overview of possibilities: obviously, what an individual chooses to include or omit is strongly influenced by what the website owner chooses to provide in the first place. In using the Kit as an analytical tool, then, the analyst first needs to itemise what resources or 'building materials' are already provided for the user.

---

**The Bricoleur's Web Kit**

**Types of activity**

- *Inclusion.* What different ideas and topics are included?
- *Allusion.* What ideas and topics are being referred to?
- *Omission.* What's left unsaid or is noticeable by its absence?
- *Adaptation.* How are materials and ideas added to or altered?
- *Arrangement.* How is everything organised on the page?

**Types of content**

- personal statistics and biographical details;
- interests, likes and dislikes;
- ideas, values, beliefs and causes;
- friends, acquaintances and personal icons (e.g. celebrities).

**Types of structure**

- written text;
- graphics – whether still or moving – and other artwork;
- sound and/or video;
- short screenfuls to long scrolls of text;
- single page or many interconnected pages;
- separate windows or frames;
- an access counter (i.e. number of people who've visited);
- a guestbook;
- links for other pages (e.g. a 'cool links' section);
- an email or chat button.

(Adapted from Chandler's own list by Thurlow *et al.*
(2004): 194. See also Chandler (2006).)

---

Choose an individual's SNS and apply the Bricoleur's Web Kit in order to analyse the choices they have made in constructing an online identity for themselves.

Both Chandler and Thurlow were writing before the most recent expansion of SNSs. Are there aspects of their checklist that no longer apply? How would you update the Web Kit in order to make it applicable to the kinds of SNS operating in contemporary environments?

(Note: there is no commentary on this activity.)

## Extension activities

1   Save some chatlogs and explore them for a chosen aspect of language use (e.g. turn-taking, humour, openings and closings, multimodality).
2   Consider what can be done via instant messaging, and what is difficult to do. Research this question by asking others what they use IM for, and try to build up a picture of its affordances.
3   Do more research on SNSs and focus on the idea of identity as subject to interpretation by asking page-owners about how they were trying to project themselves, then asking others how they 'read' the identity of those individuals.
4   Consider to what extent features of language evident in SNS wall-posts share characteristics with other kinds of e-language, such as SMS or email.
5   What functions does Twitter serve? What types of language are in evidence in tweets?
6   Explore some websites from large companies (e.g. IKEA, utility companies, technology companies) in order to look for 'chat' facilities, where you are able to ask for help in real time. How do these inter-actions work? Are they **bots**, or real individuals on the other end of the conversation? (Or real people using partly pre-programmed responses?)

# Is there anybody there?: language and identity

## Aims of this unit

- To explore issues of language and identity in online environments.
- To think about how online communication changes the way we view others, and are viewed by them.
- To link our language and communication practices online with some larger questions about information-sharing, power and privacy.

## Digital double

Eric Schmidt, the CEO of internet giant, Google, said in an interview, 'I don't believe society understands what happens when everything is available, knowable and recorded by everyone all the time' (Jenkins, 2010). To highlight this point he went on to suggest that, in the future, everyone will be entitled to change their name when they reach a certain age where they feel that they need to dissociate themselves from the documents of youthful indiscretion scattered across the web and social media websites.

Changing your name seems a rather extreme response and not an adequate solution to the problem. But what is the problem? It is common to have different presentations of yourself dependent upon the social circumstances. For example, one would commonly behave differently at work than when out on a Saturday night. Additionally, people change

**55**

over time, so the way you dress and behave now may be very different from ten years in the future or ten years in the past. Erving Goffman was writing about this in his book *The Presentation of Self in Everyday Life* as long ago as 1959 (Goffman, 1997). He discussed how we have to manage these different identities and how certain situations are bounded and contained, which enables individuals to shift between identities.

So, the change is that we no longer have such clear boundaries between these different 'faces' that Goffman discussed. In the past, it was easier to manage all these different identities. Our personal lives were more private. Memories of what happened last Saturday or last year would remain just that. Perhaps there were some very embarrassing photos of you as a child in an album gathering dust on a shelf in your parents' house. However, you would not have to worry about them being spread too widely. And anyway, you could always get rid of the evidence.

But now, increasingly, every aspect of life can be documented digitally creating an ever expanding archive. As we interact and communicate through computers, everything is logged and stored. Storage space gets bigger and bigger so there is no need to ever delete anything. And, if the data is stored online, it might be impossible to delete it.

This has led to a huge shift in how we think about 'identity'. Managing your identity is now much more complicated than it was in Goffman's time. Lyon (2007) sees identity as an ongoing task: 'Once we may have thought of our identity as a given. Now it is much more of a project, or so it seems' (2007: 179). Our identity is now not only something that is 'presented', but it is 'managed'. Online identity management is a new responsibility for the internet age.

Crandall (2007) refers to the way we are constantly paying attention to how we present ourselves as **presentational culture**. But, as you saw in the previous unit when you looked at the language of SNSs, our sense of self and our own identity is dependent not just on what we present, but also on how others perceive us. And there are so many different ways to broadcast ourselves around the globe. We may have a blog, or Twitter account, or social networking profiles, or video diary, or post videos on YouTube, or post photos on Flickr. People who want to interpret us have no limit to the amount of information they can base their impressions on.

*Activity*

As a reminder of how much interpretation we might all be doing from quite small fragments of language use, think about the email addresses below. How do you 'read' the identities of the individuals who created these linguistic tags for themselves? If one of them wrote to you for help, would any of these get a positive response from you?

What kind of email address do you have? Do you know what others think of it? Find out!

- yorkgeezerbird@hotmail.com
- pinkpetals@btinternet.com
- mitzipops@virgin.net
- gandalfsyoungerbrother@tiscali.co.uk
- twopasties@googlemail.com

(Note: there is no commentary on this activity.)

Many have embraced presentational culture, and feel isolated if they are not involved in all the global conversations made possible by new technologies. But the level of hyper-connectivity we are experiencing changes how we perceive ourselves and it changes how we perceive others. It also changes how we interact and how we get to know someone. Now it is common for two people to meet and then to 'google' each other. We have a sense that we now 'know' someone because we know what books they like, what music they listen to, what games they play, and what they had for breakfast that they had to tweet about. 'Getting to know' someone has changed and the rituals of interaction that we are used to have shifted. Additionally, 'who we are' has been in many ways reduced to 'tags' and empirical facts rather than being based on our personality or behaviour. Most profiles have a long list of 'interests' and 'groups' to which the user belongs. Our identity can quickly be placed into a socially understood category: 'I am a certain kind of person based on the identifiers I place online.' And we often use these identifiers to find people like ourselves and so, rather than expanding our social network, in many cases it narrows it.

In a culture of visibility, hiding certain aspects of yourself seems old-fashioned and even suspicious. But do we really want everyone to know everything? We are at a particular moment where we are trying to catch up culturally with what technology has enabled. This is referred to as a **cultural lag**, where technology moves and advances so quickly but, as a culture, we struggle to keep up. We can see this clearly with regard to our **digital doubles**. Many got so caught up in the excitement of being able to broadcast so much of their lives online that they did not consider what would happen when everyone could see everything.

There are serious consequences to all of this. We see people who blog about their job getting fired. Even for those who try to remain anonymous, co-workers often find out. Others lose their job when they rant about their boss on Facebook, forgetting that they had 'friended' their boss.

## *Activity*

Try going to Openbook (http://youropenbook.org/) and type in 'I hate my boss' and see what pops up. This is very personal information, which is now very public. Next, try 'so drunk' and see what you get. Do you think these people would like everyone to know this information? Did you know that this information is publicly accessible? How do you feel about this? How useful are websites like Openbook for raising awareness about these issues? Click the 'Learn why this is bad' link on Openbook. Do you agree with their stance on privacy?

(Note: there is no commentary on this activity.)

## *Activity*

How much information about you is available online? Do you have a profile on a social networking site, such as Facebook? What sort of information and data is on there? What is your own 'policy' for living your private life online? With a partner, discuss the following:

1    What are the advantages of having an online profile?
2    What sort of information and data are appropriate, in your opinion, to have online (photos, interests, email address, etc.)?
3    Do you have any issues with dealing with these different identities? Are you 'friends' with family and friends? Do you do anything to present yourself differently to these different groups?

(Note: there is no commentary on this activity.)

## And now for the other double . . .

So far, we have discussed the digital double in terms of the version of yourself that you create as your online identity, highlighting some of the problems that arise from having everything available to everyone. However, there is also a sense that we have a digital double that we cannot control – the electronic 'footprints' we leave as we go about our activities online (Mitchell, 2003; Lyon, 2007).

To consider this other form of digital double, think about all of the traces an individual leaves during the course of a day. As I wander around the internet, all of this data is recorded and accessible, often by companies who will use this data to decide what type of consumer I am, so that they can market particular products to me. For example, my purchases on Amazon create an image for Amazon of the kind of person that I am and they use that information to suggest books not just to me but to people 'like' me. Every time I use a credit card, I am giving more information about the type of person I am, how I like to spend my leisure time, where I like to shop, etc. The credit card company can then sell this information to marketing companies, who will not only use this information to build a profile of me but who will also use it to build a profile of my neighbourhood. This information will then be sold to businesses who want research data to decide where to place their shops. It will be used to determine if an up-market supermarket or a discount supermarket is placed in my area.

Then there is all the information that different government agencies have. Technology has led to three significant changes in regard to this:

- These agencies can gather information in ever more sophisticated ways.
- They can store information in ever expanding and easily accessible databases.
- And they can share this information among themselves easily and quickly.

In many ways, these advances are very helpful and have made these agencies more efficient, enabling them to target their services better. In other ways, it can have negative implications. Researchers have found that the data is not equally gathered across the population. Some, in order to receive particular services, must give more information than others. In some instances, this can lead to discrimination where individuals are judged, perhaps incorrectly, based upon their digital 'profile'. This is referred to as **social sorting**, where groups are separated and tagged based on electronic data stored.

For example, generalisations may be made that are not correct based on where you live. Governments and marketing companies gather data on particular postcodes and then make generalisations about those who live in a particular postcode. Those generalisations are then used to determine, for example, what type of services individuals receive or how much of a mortgage loan they will receive.

## Activity

Go to UpMyStreet (www.upmystreet.com) and enter your postcode. You will be given a profile about the neighbourhood in which you live. Click 'read my profile in full'. How accurate do you think this profile is?

(Note: there is no commentary on this activity.)

We may not think of it in the traditional sense of 'communicating', but we are forever 'talking' to machines. We are having conversations with machines, giving them information on us, and then they are often giving us information back. Think about getting cash. In the past, you would go to the bank and you would have to make your request for cash to a human employee of the bank. You and the bank teller would have a conversation about how much money you could have, how much money was left in your account, etc. That same conversation now occurs with a machine. Not only are our conversations increasingly with a machine, but they are now recorded. Every interaction we have with a machine creates a picture of who I am (or who I am thought to be, based on my digital 'trace').

## Activity

Ask someone, perhaps your parent, if you can take a look at their credit card bill. Try to write a story about this person just based on the data you have about them. Imagine the trips they may have gone on, or how they spent their weekend. Try to make your story as detailed as possible.

(Note: there is no commentary on this activity.)

# Extension activities

1   This unit has focused primarily on individual identity, but group identities are also expressed online. Do a survey of school or college websites and analyse how they are presenting themselves.

2   Find out how important online information is to people when they want to get to know others. Is digital identity as powerful as we are suggesting?

3   Think about times when you have experienced surprise when an individual turned out to be very different from how they seemed online. (You could actually take this question further back in time and think about people you heard on the radio, then saw a picture of.) What was it about their online identity (or voice) that made you think of them in a certain way? To get you thinking, look at the email exchange in Text 5:1 between two strangers who were preparing to meet to discuss a book project. In each case, can you guess the sex of the writers? What elements lead you to particular readings of each person? (The answer is on page 101).

## Text 5:1 Meeting a stranger

| | |
|---|---|
| **Charley**: | Hello, How about meeting for lunch to discuss this further? Would Ilkley or Manchester be suitable? |
| **Sam**: | When did you have in mind as I'm pretty booked up in August? |
| **Charley**: | One day in August ideally, but if you are busy then we could do early September. |
| **Sam**: | How about Sept 1st in Manchester? |
| **Charley**: | The 1st would be fine. Shall we say 12:30 p.m. in Piccadilly station entrance by WH Smith? I'll sort somewhere out for lunch. |
| **Sam**: | OK Charley. I'm in late fifties, bald, quite tall . . . how do I identify you? |
| **Charley**: | I'm in my early thirties with short hair and glasses. My mobile number is [number omitted], which I will have with me. See you then, Charley. |

# 'Just click here': the language of prosumerism

## Aims of this unit

- To explore how changes in web technologies are shaping our sources of information.
- To consider the positive and negative aspects of our new levels of interactivity.

## Web 2.0 and prosumers

In the early days of the internet, web pages, for the most part, were a form of one-way communication. The content was created by whoever owned and designed the website. Those who went to the website were merely 'visitors' or 'users' and there was little interaction or feedback. Much of the rhetoric around the internet when it was first introduced was that it would be democratising, that everyone would be able to get involved in world-wide conversations and debates unhindered by race, gender, age, level of education or geographical location, although initially this was rather limited by the fact that the interaction was restricted to the traditional one-way communication.

Sometime in the early 2000s, the relationship between 'producers' and 'users' shifted as web connections became faster and users were looking for more things to do online. Rather than relying upon slow dial-up connections, more and more people had broadband with unlimited connections and faster speeds. This enabled people to upload and download larger files, such as pictures, music and streaming video, as opposed to earlier websites that relied primarily upon text and low-resolution images. Additionally, software and the purchase of web space became cheaper and digital storage space grew and became less expensive. Websites began relying upon developing website templates that users could interact with to develop their own content without the need for specialised web-designing skills. This second period of the development is generally referred to as Web 2.0. This term was coined by Tim O'Reilly (of O'Reilly Media Incorporated) and refers to a trend of creating websites that are more open and participatory, focusing on getting users to interact through feedback or through generating the actual content of the website. Web 2.0, according to O'Reilly, is about 'harnessing collective intelligence' (2005).

## COLLABORATIVE SITES

So, what does that actually look like? O'Reilly gives a long list of terms that represent 'Web 1.0' and 'Web 2.0'. To take one of these, in the earlier days of the internet ('Web 1.0') we would go to the online version of a traditional encyclopaedia such as *Encyclopedia Britannica*. In Web 2.0, instead, Wikipedia (www.wikipedia.org) is preferred. With Wikipedia, individuals are not restricted to being just 'users' who must purchase information from an official and long-standing source. Instead, the users produce the information. Wikipedia is a collaborative encyclopaedia with over 91,000 active contributors (Wikipedia, 2010). This illustrates O'Reilly's point about harnessing collective intelligence, as Wikipedia is an enormous collaborative project that only exists because tens of thousands of people contribute to the website. Without these contributors there would be no Wikipedia. The developers of Wikipedia merely created the platform for the encyclopaedia to exist and manage the website to be sure that contributors abide by certain guidelines and that the website is functioning as it should.

So, what other types of websites are emblematic of Web 2.0? Blogs (such as www.blogger.com), Twitter (twitter.com), social networking sites such as Facebook (www.facebook.com), photo-sharing websites such as Flickr (www.flickr.com) and the list goes on and on. Any website that is dependent upon users contributing content and providing a platform for interaction can be considered as Web 2.0. And rather than relying upon the traditional terms of 'user' and 'producer', we have become **prosumers**. Prosumers are both 'producers' and 'consumers' and the term is an acknowledgement that it is difficult to separate groups into either of the older terms. If you have a Facebook account, you are a prosumer because you are producing your own content when engaging in activities such as posting comments on a friend's wall or uploading photos from your holiday. However, you are also a consumer of the website, using it for your entertainment and consuming the information of others in your network and receiving the advertisements posted on Facebook.

## FOLKSONOMY

Another defining characteristic of Web 2.0 applications is the creation of a **folksonomy**. This is defined by Tim O'Reilly as 'a style of collaborative categorization of sites using freely chosen keywords referred to as tags' (2005). Websites such as Flickr or YouTube are prime examples of folksonomies. For example, imagine that you have taken some photos of York over the summer and want to upload them to your Flickr account, to share with not only your family and friends but with anyone who might be interested in these photos. In order for people to find your photos you need to tag them so that they will come up in a search for a particular term.

In the past, items would have to be placed in one file or folder on your computer. You would have to decide: do you want to put your photos in a photo album of photos from your summer when you travelled to many places, or would you put the photos in an album just of photos of York but that might include photos from a broader time span? With tagging, you can now classify these photos into as many categories as you like. So you could tag all of the photos 'Summer', 'York' and 'England'. And then you could give certain photos even more specific tags such as 'garden', 'museum', 'sunset', 'rain', etc. This way, if someone wanted to see photos of York, your photos and all the photos of all other users tagged York would pop up in a search. Or if they just wanted photos of rain, they could get the photos that you and others took in the rain.

Flickr, then, works as an enormous database of photos that can be searched by tags. There are so many photos uploaded to Flickr that it would be impossible to find a particular theme or photo without these tags, which form a folksonomy and make Flickr easy to use.

## The debate over Web 2.0: the positives

The development of Web 2.0 can be interpreted both positively and negatively. The positive aspects of Web 2.0 have been promoted by many web entrepreneurs, such as Tim O'Reilly, and bloggers/writers, such as Clay Shirky and Charles Leadbeater. Charles Leadbeater has published a book entitled *We-think: Mass innovation, not mass production* (2008a) and you can grasp his perspective from this title. He believes that 'Ideas take life when they are shared. That is why the web is such a potent platform for creativity and innovation' (2008b). Clay Shirky, similarly, focuses on the powerful potential of **prosumption** in his essay 'RIP the consumer: 1900–1999', where he states, 'In the age of the Internet, no one is a passive consumer anymore because everyone is a media outlet' (Shirky, 2000). These writers focus on the enormous potential of the internet to be used as a tool for large-scale collaborative projects. From this viewpoint, individuals can work together to create things that they would not be able to create on their own. Or, when individuals pull together they can have a powerful influence to challenge institutions and bring about social change. Wikipedia is certainly an aspect of this. It is an enormous encyclopedia of information and, for the most part, the information is very good. Because there are so many people collaborating, inaccurate information is generally corrected.

Examples of online political activism also illustrate the collaborative power of Web 2.0. There are many online activism websites to choose from but, as a single example, look at Avaaz.org (www.avaaz.org). According to the website, the group has 5.5 million members all around the world and is 'the largest global web movement in history'. Through the website, the group raises money for various causes, generates global petitions on various issues, and has organised rallies, vigils, marches and online events. It is an example of how the internet can be used to bring people together to work towards a particular social or political cause and how much more powerful these large organisations can be compared to individuals working alone.

## The debate over Web 2.0: the negatives

Let's look at Clay Shirky's statement again and consider some of the implications of this. The comment that everyone has the potential to be a media outlet refers to individuals creating blogs, uploading home videos to YouTube, and creating adaptations of stories on websites such as FanFiction (www.fanfiction.net). Individuals can challenge media institutions by creating their own content. This is particularly powerful with news. Blogs and Twitter allow individuals to challenge the official media coverage of issues and events. In the Iranian elections in 2009, and the subsequent protests, the version of events offered by the state media was challenged by **citizen journalists** who used blogs and Twitter to mobilise protests and to broadcast to the rest of the world a different perspective from that of the official state media.

On the other hand, if everyone is blogging and twittering how can we, as users, filter through all of this 'noise'? How do we distinguish between fact and opinion? How do we navigate through individual biases? How do we determine if a source is reputable? Andrew Keen has been a very vocal critic of Web 2.0 and focuses on the negative aspects of all these individual media outlets. In his book *The Cult of the Amateur*, he states:

> Blogs have become so dizzyingly infinite that they've under-mined our sense of what is true and what is false, what is real and what is imaginary. These days, kids can't tell the difference between credible news by objective professional journalists and what they read on joeshmoe.blogspot.com. For these Generation Y utopians, every posting is just another person's version of the truth; every fiction is just another person's version of the facts.
>
> (Keen, 2007: 3)

## *Activity*

With a partner, discuss how you find out about what's going on in the world. Where do you go for news? Do you go to the internet, television, or radio? What websites do you prefer? How do you determine if a source is reliable?

(Note: there is no commentary on this activity.)

## THE DEMAND FOR INFORMATION

With everyone producing their own content online and this proliferation of opinions and conversations taking place, it is increasingly difficult to wade through everything that is available. However, many of these web-sites are dependent upon individuals creating content and uploading their thoughts and the content of their everyday life to share with the world. Social networking websites such as Facebook are only successful if we put stuff up there. And there is an ever increasing demand for more and more information. We want to know and consume more and more of each other's daily life from twittering about your breakfast, blogging about your break-up, uploading home videos of your cat, and sharing photos from the party on Saturday night. These websites merely provide a platform and a space for sharing all of this. The important thing for these websites is that they are easy and inviting to use. If they didn't have subscribers, they would just be empty spaces.

So, actually, we are doing all the work! You can look at this phenomenon positively and see the powerful challenge to governments and biased media by citizen journalists. Or, you could interpret it negatively and consider that these citizen journalists are now doing the work of traditional journalists but without getting paid.

Mainstream news organisations are increasingly depending upon the public to give them tips on news stories or to send in photographs or mini-reports on events. These organisations can promote themselves as being more inclusive but, on the other hand, they do not need to employ so many reporters if the public is willing and happy to do the job for free. According to Lev Manovich, in his essay 'The practice of everyday (media) life' (2008), the popularity of Web 2.0 and what is referred to as **social media** is driven by the business interests of these various websites and also by the consumer electronics industry. These websites make money by selling advertising space on their sites.

However, there have to be users using the website to attract advertisers. Additionally, they make money from selling our data. Again, think of Facebook: when you spend hours in an evening uploading photos and tagging your friends and joining groups and adding ever more detail to your profile, Facebook will make money from your hours of effort. You are working for Facebook for free. Meanwhile, Facebook will promote this as evidence of the power of the community of Facebook users and returning to O'Reilly's idea of 'harvesting collective intelligence'. Facebook is now translated into many languages. Rather than employing a huge number of translators, 300,000 Facebook users helped translate the website using its translation application. They did this for free.

## Interactive advertising: just click here

All of these social media applications rely on users in order to make money. Often they make money through selling advertising. You may have already studied the language aspects of more traditional advertising, but online advertising offers a whole new range of creative possibilities for marketing a product. Compared to traditional print or television advertising there is less of a space restriction, which allows the advertisements to be more dynamic and, most significantly, to be interactive.

Look at the advertisement in Text 6:1, which was taken from Facebook.

## Text 6:1 Cobra

The effectiveness of online advertisements is measured by the number of people who click on the advert. The key is to get the users to engage with the advert in some way so that the company can be sure that the advertisement is getting attention. The advertisement in Text 6:1 uses language in particular ways to encourage interactivity. It creates a sense of inclusivity and community that seems inviting, allowing us access to this fun community that enjoys curry and Cobra beer.

The advertisement wants you to feel like you have a relationship with the company and other people who enjoy the product. It relies upon the pronoun 'we': 'We're big curry fans. If you are too, join us . . .'. It wants you to join the 'gang' and enjoy a curry. To further emphasise this, it then asks you a playful question about what type of curry lover you are: 'How do you make yours?' The key is that it draws you in to respond to the question. As you can see above, when this advertisement was grabbed from Facebook in June of 2010, 5,472 people had voted. That shows the power of the advertisement to get people to engage.

However, that is not the extent of the information that Cobra receives from this ad. Take a look at the information page for Facebook Ads (www.facebook.com/adsmarketing – current as of January 2011). Advertisers can target their ads to particular groups within particular **demographics** or interests. The effectiveness of the ad can be similarly measured. Facebook reports to the businesses a great deal of information about the people who click on the advertisement – those 5,472 people who responded to the question about curry, for example. Facebook provides the companies with information about those who click, including age, gender, location, interests, movies and books. This is a very vivid demonstration of how all of that information put up on Facebook makes the company money.

Compared with paying for a traditional print ad in a magazine, Facebook interactive ads allow for a tremendous amount of information to help businesses target those who would be receptive to the product. However, they can only measure if the advertisement is effective and see who is interested in it if they interact with the advert. This is why companies try to develop novel ways of getting viewers to interact with their adverts.

## *Activity*

Try to find some other interactive ads online. Social networking websites are a good place to start, but many popular blogs and online magazines that rely on advertising for money will also have ads. Examine how these ads use language to encourage viewers to click on the ad and interact with it.

(Note: there is no commentary on this activity.)

## Web 2:0 case studies: YouTube and LOLcats

To conclude this unit we will take a look at some examples of social media that are tremendously popular and emblematic of the success of Web 2.0. What is unusual about these websites is the scale of interactivity that takes place on them. While some critics have suggested that the internet and Web 2.0 have led to a decrease in writing and language use, these websites, in the scale of conversations constantly taking place and the sophistication of these conversations, counter this claim.

## YOUTUBE

YouTube is a video uploading website. Created in 2005, it has quickly become a critical part of online interactions. Two billion videos are watched every day around the world and, every minute, 24 hours of video are uploaded (YouTube, 2010). YouTube is an example of both the positives and negatives of Web 2.0, with a vast range of material, from grainy home-made video clips to professional advertisements uploaded by the companies themselves.

Thankfully, videos are tagged, creating a detailed folksonomy that enables users to filter through all the material. YouTube offers a bit of everything for everyone. Individuals may upload a home video, a parody of a mainstream video, or archive video footage from TV from decades ago. It is an impressive collaborative history project in itself. If you type in Margaret Thatcher (Prime Minister of the United Kingdom from 1979 to 1990), you receive 2,490 videos, mostly clips of speeches and interviews that have been uploaded even though most are decades old. In this sense, we can see how YouTube is an invaluable source for primary material, to watch historic moments for yourself rather than merely reading about them in a textbook.

The most significant aspect of YouTube is that it connects the world and brings people into a conversation on a global scale. And those conversations can be about anything and everything. For example, you search for a favourite topic, cats on a treadmill (search terms 'cat' and 'treadmill'). You receive 1,120 video results. You choose to watch a home video about a cat named November who explores the treadmill. This video has been watched 816,602 times. Additionally, the video has 1,387 comments posted. It is an enormous conversation with individuals responding to each other and, in general, having a global conversation about this cat walking on a treadmill. And that is just one of 1,120 videos of a cat on a treadmill. This gives you an idea of the scale of the conversations that take place on YouTube.

Once individuals have registered on the site and chosen a pseudonym to use, they can take part in the discussion on YouTube. Obviously, one problem that arises when you have so many people participating at once is that it is difficult to monitor what is being said. Unfortunately, you might see that some people are expressing in fairly inappropriate language that they do not enjoy watching cats on treadmills as much as you do. This highlights one of the problems of this great new world where we can all talk to each other; sometimes it is very difficult to filter out all of the language that you would rather avoid. And because people are anonymous on sites such as YouTube, many feel that they have the freedom to say anything they would like, no matter how offensive.

71

## LOLCATS

Our second example of social media is **LOLcats**. There are many different versions and permutations of the trend of LOLcats, but it started out with users uploading photos of cats and then other users adding humorous captions to the photos. However, this phenomenon grew rapidly to a massive scale and a particular dialect developed on these websites, where the captions were intentionally written in grammatically incorrect English to suggest that the captions were written by non-native English speakers. They also borrowed some phrases and conventions from video games.

What started out as a joke became increasingly popular and sophisticated and led to the development of **LOLspeak**. The most popular LOLcat website is 'I Can Has Cheezeburger' (icanhascheezburger.net), which also includes a whole list of permutations on the idea, with different pages for adding captions to photos of dogs, celebrities, sports images, and the very popular 'FAIL blog' and 'Engrish' websites. Like YouTube, the images are tagged to create a folksonomy and users comment on the photos. Most importantly, users add their own captions to the photos.

Users vote on those captions and then the most popular caption is what is shown on the main website with the photo. There are many conventions and trends that the users perpetuate such as 'monorail kitteh' (when cats appear to be on some sort of track), 'nom nom nom' (when a cat is enjoying eating something), 'ur doing it wrong' (a joke that something is being done incorrectly or a 'fail'), and 'ceiling cat' (a cat that looks through a hole in the ceiling and is considered to be omniscient and always watching) (Nakagawa and Unebasami, 2008).

Text 6:2 is an example of what a LOLcat might look like.

The website offers a brief tutorial on LOLspeak, but it is difficult to grasp the conventions without just spending some time looking at the captions. The basic idea is to try to think of something amusing to say to go along with the picture. Then change it and put in spelling and grammatical errors. For example, it is very common to change an 's' to a 'z' as in 'cheezeburger' instead of 'cheeseburger', or to use 'i iz' instead of 'I am'. Next, it helps to add lots of exclamations and speech noises to create a sense of voice, like the 'aargh!' in Text 6:2. Then there are many popular phrases, some of which were given above, but there are many others, for example:

- 'i is hidin. you no seek.'
- 'im in ur dishwasher, waitin fer my showr.'

(www.icanhascheezeburger.net)

### Text 6:2 I Iz Pirate

aargh! i iz pirate. giv us ur cheezburgurz and katnip.

The LOLcats phenomenon has become so well known that, in the most recent general election in the UK (May 2010), some of the tabloid press used the idea in satirising Nick Clegg, the then leader of the Liberal Democrats: photographs of him were captioned using 'LOLcleggz'. Here is an example, commenting on his change of policy on university students' tuition fees:

I HAZ MADE YOU A COMMITMENT TO SCRAP TUTITION FEES BUT I EATED IT ☹

Despite media use of this kind of playful new language, there are critical voices in the media lamenting the appearance of new linguistic forms. This will be discussed in more detail in the next unit. So, for example, when individuals shorten words and vary their spellings so that they are easier to txt, some commentators claim to see a degradation of the English language in the process. At first glance, LOLspeak may appear to be an example of this degradation and demonstrate how young people no longer know how to write 'properly'. On the other hand, LOLspeak could be interpreted as evidence that language is thriving and alive. The spelling and grammatical errors in LOLspeak are not accidents or mistakes, and users have to have considerable expertise in language structure and interpretation in order to make unconventional forms communicate. LOLspeak is a playful exercise with language. It is knowingly poking fun at those who assert that language must remain static and we must adhere to a strict version of 'correctness'.

LOLspeak is a part of a long tradition of playing with language for humour. It is also a vibrant example of the power of social media and Web 2.0. The internet has allowed us to connect with others more than ever before in these global forms of interaction. Our use of language is ever adapting and new words related to technology use enter the dictionary every year. Inevitably, there will be those who embrace the creative potential that is on offer and there will be those who lament the changes and wish to adhere to more traditional use of language and more traditional power relationships between media producers and users.

## Activity

Try to make your own LOLcat with Text 6:3.

(Note: there is no commentary on this activity.)

## Text 6:3 Cat

## Extension activity

This unit has suggested a number of websites and sources of information that need to be explored carefully. Working with a friend or in a group, take one of the sites or information sources and spend some time using and reflecting on what you find. Then prepare a presentation for your class or study group on your findings.

# Shock! Horror!
# The representation of
# new technologies

## Aims of this unit

- To explore the way new technologies are described in the public discourses around us.
- To develop skills in analysing the way representations are constructed.

## What is representation?

In Unit 1, it was noted that fear about new communication technologies is not a new phenomenon. However, fear is not the only attitude we express towards new technologies: you saw, again in Unit 1, that when you looked back to your own history of acquiring new communication tools, there was a variety of attitudes and experiences to report. It shouldn't be surprising, therefore, to find a complex mix of different kinds of stories when we look across our public media for accounts of technology.

Thinking about **representation** involves us in looking at different reports and stories, while believing that no one report or story is 'the truth'. Representation is all about how things appear to be, rather than believing that this is 'how things really are'. At a literal level, representation means 'standing in place of something', so the stories we have about technology stand in place of reality. In other words, they make up our reality for us.

Representations are embedded in discourses, or ways of talking and writing. Examples of different discourses can be found in this INTERTEXT series – for example, the language of sport, the language of politics, the language of science, the language of work. Each of these books tries to capture something of the patterns that are present in an area of language use, so in each case readers become not only acquainted with a different discourse, but also able to **critique** it.

## REPRESENTATIONS OF TECHNOLOGY IN ADVERTISING

The advertising of technology has a long history of what some computer scientists have called 'high tech, high touch' (Naisbitt, 1982), which means that, because technology is potentially frightening to consumers, the marketing message has to be about comfort and reassurance. Comfort can come in many forms, of course. One common theme is that new communication tools can enable us to have more connections with our friends and family, so you see advertisements that stress the 'human intimacy factor' of new tools, showing their capacity for person-to-person inter-action. At the time of writing, BT's 'Adam and Jane' story has been running in British TV ads for five years, showing a supposedly twenty-first-century family (divorce and remarriage, stepchildren, adults having to work away from home) and highlighting the role different communication tools could have in keeping the family together.

Comfort isn't necessarily sexy, though. A further common strand of advertising discourse is around the 'good looks' of the new tools, promoting them as stylish and desirable. Sometimes, this leads to highly gendered ads. For example, an ad for Trium mobile phones in 1999 had the hook 'The pleasure of conversation' against the backdrop of a naked woman posing in the style of a sex chatline advert. The advertising copy talked about the shapely curves of the phone and its responsive nature, which reacted to 'a flick of the thumb'. At that point in time, advertisers may well have been aiming at a fairly privileged male market, while mobile phones now are more competitively priced and affordable for most consumers, at least in Western societies. However, representations of gender haven't necessarily gone away, as you may already have seen if you researched this as a Unit 1 'Extension activity'.

A further common theme in advertising, not just phones but communication tools of all kinds, is that of fitting into the demands of modern lifestyles, with our need for speed of communication, reliability and ease of use. The ultimate accolade for a piece of technology is for us to feel that it's so much a part of our lives that we can't do without it –

this was the focus of an activity in Unit 2, where you were asked what your choice for a 'desert island' gadget would be.

For example, in 2007, BT's 'More power to you' campaign used txting language to advertise its new Equinox phone, suggesting that it was up to date with the language its consumers were using:

> Txts r gr8.
> If only u cld snd them frm
> Yr home phone.
> R. But u cn.
> Thx 2 BT Equinox 1200.

And a Carphone Warehouse advert in 2010 asks 'How did you get through the day without Android apps?' (Android is currently a new operating system), suggesting that, if you haven't bought an Android phone yet, you are missing out on a technology that is indispensable.

### *Activity*

Focusing on your own mobile phone, try to answer the following:

* Why did you buy the phone you have?
* Is there a new type of phone you would like and, if so, how has it been marketed?
* Do you think phone advertising is gendered? Can you give some examples?
* Go online (or use any available magazine advertising you have) and collect some examples of mobile phone advertising. Can you see any of the themes mentioned here? Are there further themes? Pool your results with others, if possible, to get a good understanding of the representations that emerge.

(Note: there is no commentary on this activity.)

## REPRESENTATIONS OF TECHNOLOGY IN NEWS STORIES

Representations in news stories also cover a range of themes, and many different technologies. Stories tend to be either positive or negative in their representations. Taken overall, for every scare story, there's a story about the miraculous power of new forms of communication. While there is no simple account possible that all points in one direction, one thing is for sure – new technologies provide huge amounts of column inches for journalists.

The titles below are from a range of articles collected over the last ten years. After each of the titles, there is a brief summary of what the article covered (unless the title is self-explanatory). If you want to read the full article in each case, you will probably be able to find some of them by searching the relevant newspaper's archives.

The different sections below show you different discourses about technology – in other words, these are themes that are repeated over and over again. Sometimes this level of discourse is distinguished from the work of analysing a single text, which is also called discourse analysis. For example, James Paul Gee (1990) terms the definition of discourse that tries to achieve an overview by focusing on many examples 'discourse with a capital D', to distinguish it from a detailed analysis of a single text.

## 1 The power of information

The articles below feature different contexts and people, but share a common theme of power – the power of state or corporate forces to know about individuals, the power of individuals to resist surveillance, and the power of technology to reach mass audiences.

'CCTV in pools "will be a lifesaver"'
*The Independent*, 25 January 2001
A new kind of CCTV system detects swimmers in difficulty – cameras are underwater as well as above. The article expresses concern about individual privacy.

'Tesco tests spy chip technology'
*The Guardian Business*, 19 July, 2003
A new kind of tag – radio frequency identity (RFID) tag – is being put into everyday items and, when these items are bought by customers, could be used to track the whereabouts of the consumers as well as the products.

'Heads spy on teachers'
*The Times Educational Supplement* (*TES*) 10 April 2006
A new generation of surveillance cameras (with microphones) is being installed in classrooms.

'Should computers be made to forget?'
Wired Campus, *The Chronicle of Higher Education*, 1 May 2007
This is about the dangers of having permanent records: if we archive everything we do, will we be too nervous to be spontaneous?

'Move over JK, this is the world's most-read author'
*The Independent*, 21 July 2007
This challenges the idea of traditional publishing – a blog written by a young Chinese author has millions more readers than J.K. Rowling, author of the *Harry Potter* books.

'German supermarket chain Lidl accused of snooping on staff'
*The Guardian*, 27 March 2008
CCTV cameras are recording workers in their staffrooms, including while on their mobile phones. Toilet visits are rationed. Women who have their periods are allowed more visits but have to wear special headbands.

'Chinese couple to sue metro over stolen kiss'
*The Times Online*, 22 January 2008
A couple kissing in a Chinese metro system are recorded on CCTV and put up on YouTube, with sniggering voices of surveillance workers audible. They are taking the metro company to court.

## Text 7:1 It's gr8 wot u can do by txt

Front page of *Times2* (displayed on a phone), 4 December 2008.
A British surgeon saves the life of an injured man in the Congo, Africa, by getting instructions on how to conduct a major operation via text from an expert in the UK.

'Call for safeguards over Big Brother database'
*The Independent*, 10 January 2009
A database has been created to collect our communications, including all txts and emails.

'Get street wise – Big Brother is googling you'
*London Evening Standard*, 25 March 2009
The journalist Will Self raises privacy issues about Google Street View.

'Goodbye cruel web: legal row as social networkers escape in "suicide machine"'
*The Times*, 23 January 2010
Facebook tries to stop another site (called 'the suicide machine') from helping people deactivate their accounts.

'Silence in the street: spy mikes are listening'
*The Times*, 20 June 2010
New types of CCTV camera can record our conversations from long distances away.

'Wikileaks founder who torments the Pentagon comes out of shadows'
*The Independent*, 10 July 2010
Julian Assange, who runs a website publicising classified information, appears publicly for the first time.

## 2 Children

These articles all focus on children's use of technology.

'Text-mad children turning to drink'
*Metro*, 17 February 2005
This article, and the one below, are reproduced and discussed – see Text 7:2 on page 89.

'Texts "cause more harm than dope"'
*Metro*, 22 April 2005

'Social websites harm children's brains: Chilling warning to parents from top neuroscientist'
*MailOnline*, 24 February 2009

'Mobiles linked to raised risk of brain cancer in children'
*Daily Mail*, 22 September 2008

'One in five children has Web meeting'
*Metro*, 28 May 2008

## 3 Language, learning and changes in social practices

These articles cover issues about change – language change, and the social changes that accompany new ways of communicating.

'Now chat is where it's at'
*The Independent*, 10 May 1999
The article claims that email is being superseded by instant messenger systems, which were new at the time.

'Is the handwritten letter a thing of the past?'
Historical Notes, *The Independent*, 13 October 1999

'Internet unplugged'
*The Observer*, 12 December 1999
This introduces the new idea of mobile technologies.

'My summer hols wr CWOT. B4, we usd 2 go 2NY 2C my bro, his GF & 3 :-@ kds FTF'
'Is this written in text or just bad spelling?'
*The Times Higher Education Supplement*, 19 September 2003
The txt previously featured as a tabloid headline, supposedly written by a school pupil. (It was later claimed to be a fake.) The *THES* author debates the issues of skills, standards and generational differences.

'English exam hit by epidemic of street language'
*The Independent*, 17 September 2005
This article is reproduced and discussed – see Text 7:3 on page 000.

'Texting teenagers are proving "more literate than ever before"'
*The Times*, 31 October 2005
A new report claims that standards of literacy have risen among the age group that comprises regular txters.

'The pain and perils of Blackberry thumb'
*The Times*, 2 October 2007
Mobile devices are blamed for causing repetitive strain injuries.

'Computers blamed as reading standards slump'
*The Independent*, 29 November 2007

'How the Queen became very well connected'
*The Observer*, 23 December 2007
The Queen is said to have a mobile phone and an iPod.

'IC u r worried about student literacy. Don't b'
*The Times Higher Education Supplement*, 28 May 2008
A book review of David Crystal's *Txtng: the gr8 db8*.

'How Wikipedia can help schoolchildren'
*The Times*, 29 May 2008
Wikipedia is to be part of the school curriculum in New South Wales, Australia, as a way to exemplify the 'global village'.

'Grappling with the digital divide'
*The Times Higher Education Supplement*, 14 August 2008
Students may have better digital literacy skills than their tutors.

'Text-message spelling in school? Have we gone mad? Why does everything have to be made so easy for children today?'
Education Quandary, *The Independent*, 25 September 2008

'Do you speak geek?'
*The Independent*, 18 February 2009
An account of some of the new in-group references being used in computer contexts.

'Pain of dial-and-walk'
*The London Paper* (freesheet), date unknown
People are having accidents because they are texting as they walk.

'Texting is making English a foreign language'
*The Daily Telegraph*, 12 August 2009
The writer claims that literature 'will become as abbreviated as teenagers' attention spans'.

## 4 Crime

In these examples, consider to what extent the technology is implicated in the crimes described; and also, what crimes have been committed in some cases.

Internet chatroom led M&S model to her death
*London Evening Standard*, 25 July 2006
A woman is killed by her partner, whom she met initially in a chatroom. Online he was a very different character from how he was face to face.

'Bloggers name and shame MySpace suicide neighbours'
*The Independent*, 24 November 2007
Local people take revenge on an adult woman who impersonated a boy, started a relationship with a neighbour's teenage daughter, then dumped her. The daughter then hanged herself.

'Secrets found in text messages'
*The Times Higher Education Supplement*, 18 September 2008
A report about forensic linguistics and its role in uncovering a murderer's fake txts. He sent txts impersonating his victim in order to give himself an alibi.

'Facebook "friends" hijacked in scam'
*Metro*, 11 November 2008
People are impersonating others on Facebook in order to obtain money by trading on friendships.

## 5 Technology and identity

These articles are about how individuals can behave differently, or create a new identity for themselves, in a virtual environment. An alternative view might be that people's 'real' identities are amplified online.

'How e-mail puts us in a flaming bad temper'
*The Independent*, 2 April 1999
Early coverage of flaming in emails.

'Free your mind – ban all e-mails'
*Metro*, 5 March 2001
Some businesses are suggesting an email-free Friday, with the idea that other modes of communication are more creative.

'What message are you sending out?'
*Daily Mail*, 3 December 2004
How different email styles may be read by others.

'Party girl's e-mail goes round the world'
*The Independent*, 26 August 2006
A girl comes across as a terrible snob, telling party invitees how to dress and behave at her party. The initial recipients of her email broadcast it globally.

'Penguin is the Ping of blogs'
*Metro*, 28 May 2008
A playful story about a penguin who has his own blog (obviously written by a human being).

'Diddit – the new website for the online boasting community'
*The Independent*, 22 February 2009
A site where people compete with each other about their achievements.

## 6 Personal relationships

These articles all address how individuals have incorporated new technologies into their personal lives.

'Sorry, but itz ova'
*Metro*, 19 November 2003
The ethics of ending relationships by text.

'We met by flexting* . . . now we're engaged'
*The Sun*, 28 December 2007
An article about flirting by txt (flexting).

'Husband sacks wife by email'
*Daily Express*, 23 February 2008
The husband ran the company where his wife was employed.

'First online love match hits 25 yrs'
*Metro*, 20 May 2008
This is about a couple who met via very early technology – CompuServe in 1983.

'The fall-out when two worlds collide'
*The Independent*, 16 November 2008
A couple divorce because of the behaviour of the husband's avatar on Second Life.

'Facebook "friends" are fine, but the more we chat the less we say'
*The Independent*, 22 February 2009
The writer argues that our online networks are superficial and don't match real-life friendships.

'Wiki-dumped ex has eBay revenge'
*Metro*, date unknown
The girlfriend of Jimmy Wales (founder of Wikipedia) sells his clothes on eBay after he ended their relationship on Wikipedia.

The news extracts do not give an exhaustive view of all representations of technology: they are a sample of articles from a small range of newspapers based in the UK. The coverage of technology and its associated issues will certainly have been much more extensive than this collection suggests, particularly if you think about all the different news media around the world.

To help you review what you have read so far, here is a summary of the themes that have been covered:

Technology and:

1    power – of the state, of individuals;
2    children's use of technology;
3    changes in language and social behaviour;
4    crime;
5    identity;
6    relationships.

These categories are quite fluid, and some of the articles could go in more than one category.

*Activities*

- Thinking first about what has been covered, what would you say the collection shows about our cultural concerns and preoccupations in general?
- Take one particular theme from the six listed, and focus in more detail about how that issue or area has been represented. Even though the articles have only been summarised, you should still have been able to get a sense of how the story has been treated from reading the headlines in each case.
- Research one or two of these articles more fully by searching for the full version online.
- Search both online and in paper-based publications (newspapers, magazines, etc.) for more contemporary stories about technology. Do your searches bear out the categories above, or are there more categories that should be included? Are the stories similar in their viewpoints to the attitudes shown in this collection?
- If you can speak a language other than English, search some further news media outlets for reports about new technologies. To what extent is their coverage similar to what you have seen here?

(Note: there is no commentary on these activities.)

## Discourse with a small 'd'

The final section of this unit will focus on the analysis of individual texts, printed in Texts 7:2 and 7:3.

The ability to focus in detail on how texts work is an essential aspect of understanding representation thoroughly.

## *Activity*

Use these guideline questions to help you analyse the texts printed below:

1 Focusing just on the headlines, what aspects of language use reveal the attitudes of the writers to their stories?
2 How does the headline in each case fit with the story and its factual claims?
3 How are 'expert voices' used to claim authority?
4 If research is quoted, is it clear what has been researched and found?
5 What concepts and arguments are being proposed by each of the writers?

Note: there is a commentary on this activity at the back of the book.

## Text 7:2a Text-mad children

# Text-mad children turning to drink

TEENAGERS addicted to their mobile phones are more likely to drink and smoke, a study suggests. Constant texting and non-stop calls are seen as rebellious by 14 to 16-year-olds and smoking and drinking is just another part of 'street culture', psychologists say. Yet the self-styled rebels may not be quite as anti-Establishment as they believe. Many are middle-class and rely on part-time jobs and pocket money to fund their habits. A study of 3,500 youngsters in Finland, which has similar rates of mobile phone use to Britain, found teenagers spent up to four hours a day on the phone, according to a report in the scientific Journal of Adolescence.

Text 7:2b Text-mad children

# Texts 'cause more harm than dope'

## BY GEORGINA LITTLEJOHN

TEXTING and e-mailing causes more than twice as much damage to the brain as smoking marijuana, new research claims.

Tapping messages into a mobile phone or on a computer keyboard temporarily knocks ten points off the user's IQ. But smoking a joint reduces the user's IQ by just four points, said psychologists who term the cause as 'Infomania'.

Employees see a noticeable drop in IQ because they are constantly being distracted from what they should be doing, according to the study from technology giant Hewlett Packard.

The brain finds it hard to cope with juggling with lots of tasks at once, reducing its overall effectiveness.

'This is a very real and widespread phenomenon,' said psychologist Dr Glenn Wilson, of the University of London.

'Infomania, if unchecked, will damage a worker's performance by reducing their mental sharpness.'

While modern technology can have big benefits, too much use can be damaging to a person's mind, not to mention their work and social life.

More than six in ten workers admit they are addicted to checking their e-mail and text messages so much they look at work-related ones even when at home. Half

Dumbing down: Texting 'can reduce your IQ'

said they always responded to an e-mail as soon as possible and one in five would interrupt a meeting to do so.

It may also damage the user's image among friends, as nine out of ten people think those who interrupt what they are doing to answer calls are rude.

Hewlett Packard said that firms which give staff gadgets to keep in touch should produce guidelines for their use.

Its best-practice tips include using 'dead time', such as when travelling, to read messages and check e-mails, and turning devices off in meetings.

HP commercial manager David Smith said: 'The research suggests that we are in danger of being caught up in a 24-hour "always on" society.'

## Text 7:3 Epidemic of street language

# English exam hit by epidemic of street language

**By Richard Garner**
Education Editor

**◻ Street usage found in GCSEs**

- **"gonna" for "going to"**
- **"m8" for "mate"**
- **"aint" for "are not"**
- **"wanna" for "want to"**
- **"u" for "you"**
- **"shouda" for "should have"**
- **"i" for "I"**

An epidemic of the use of street-culture language broke out in this year's GCSE English exam essays, according to examiners.

A report by the Edexcel exam board said there was "a surprising number of lapses" in standard English. It issued a reminder to teachers that they should discourage pupils from using "street language and text style", adding: "Most answers require formal expression [of language]."

"Many concerns were expressed by examiners about elementary errors, often appearing in the work of apparently able candidates," the report continued.

"At this level it is almost unforgivable for a candidate to use a lower case for the first person pronoun – and yet in occasional answers this mistake was repeated throughout essays." It added that the use of street and text language "appeared with surprisingly regularity in the work of candidates who clearly aspired to at least a C grade".

"Most answers require formal expression but – even when an informal register or style is appropriate – candidates should remain aware of the examination context and, in particular, should not use street language and text style," it said.

There is rising concern about pupils' writing skills, especially among boys. National curriculum test results for 11-year-olds showed boys' writing standards had fallen this year. Only 55 per cent reached the level expected of an 11-year-old by the time they left primary school, the results showed.

Ministers have set up an urgent review of the national literacy hour in primary schools – which is being conducted by a former chief primary schools inspector, Jim Rose. Many educationalists are now arguing that he should also investigate ways of improving writing standards.

The Edexcel report said spelling was "in general inconsistent" and "variety of vocabulary and of sentence structure is often limited". It went on: "Punctuation errors continue to be widespread, with the absence or misuse of the apostrophe a recurrent problem."

However, it added: "Some examiners felt that this year they had encountered an improvement in the overall structure of candidates' writing."

# Commentaries

Unit one, p. 1

It is of course not possible to anticipate exactly what will emerge from this activity. However, certain common themes and experiences are often in evidence, for example:

- enjoyment of new learning experiences;
- feeling proud of owning something that others might envy; and/or
- feeling frustrated and envious that others were given greater freedom and licence, or more sophisticated items;
- being able to do new things that were not possible before;
- professional advancement through an enhancement of skills;
- trial and error in the form of 'test runs' with the new technology;
- learning from others about how to manage and use new tools;
- a sense of group membership and exploration of identities;
- unhappy memories – for example, of not understanding how things worked;
- the importance of particular forms of language use.

# Unit one (Texts 1:3 and 1:4), pp. 6/7

### What strategies are the advertisers using in order to sell these toys?

The toys are packaged using bright colours, with images of happy, smiling children. There are many different voices in the text, including that of the child ('My first soft mobile phone'), a puppy 'friend' talking to the child ('I can learn your name'), a learning expert ('See your child's play . . .), and even the phone itself ('Try Me! Press a number!'). Notions of audience are interesting, as clearly children of three months or even 18 months cannot read. The text, then, appears to address the child but is actually aimed at parents, but often via a 'fun' voice to suggest excitement and engagement. A direct address to parents, however, can be found on the warning label of 'British Voices' attached to the Leap Frog box. American parents are being warned that the toy uses voices with British accents to count and sing.

### What claims are being made about the skills children learn by using these toys?

More skills are claimed by the Leap Frog phone than the My First Soft Mobile. However, the latter offers a 'mirror to encourage self-recognition', and 'gentle sounds' of electronic nursery tunes plus a phone ringtone. The picture presents a happy child listening to music, and the toy offers a hook for attaching to prams. Like the teddy bear in the brand image, the toy is being presented as a tactile experience – a toy 'made from super-soft fabric perfect for little hands'. Leap Frog presents itself as a 'Learning Path', which suggests a planned trajectory of skills development where a child will naturally progress. The advertising copy talks of learning 'conversational skills' (voices on the toy say 'hi', 'hello' and 'bye-bye', but not much else that could be termed conversation). It also seems to think that voicemails and ringtones can 'set imaginations free'. The side of the packaging positions Leap Frog as sharing the parental hope 'to be there every step of the way'. The phone is said to 'inspire imaginations and encourage new discoveries'.

### What messages about the world are being communicated by these toys?

Toys such as these prefigure the real phones that children will begin to use as they grow up, and serve to market the idea of phones as consumer products. In being a part of the child's world, the toys make phones seem a natural accessory, a must-have part of the environment. While the toys claim to offer valuable experiences – tactile skills, conversational skills – in reality the toys are early marketing opportunities for getting young consumers to feel positive about their products from the very start of life.

## Unit two, p. 13

These are some of the factors that might have come up in your discussion. Rather than going through each possible communication tool, the notes below summarise aspects that are associated with several forms of new communication.

These points have been informed by university students' group discussions and research over the last six years. Remember, though, that technology changes fast, so there may be aspects that are out of date; you will certainly be able to add to these points, so don't regard the lists below as definitive.

*Possible affordances*:
- inexpensive (but remember the hidden costs of the infrastructures for new technologies, such as internet service providers and phone company charges);
- fast communication possible; high level of interactivity;
- mobility and accessibility;
- can have international, global scope (but remember global differences in both economic factors and also issues of censorship);
- asynchronous tools (i.e. where participants don't have to be online simultaneously) can allow readers to digest information privately;
- people can create a new identity online, so can be liberating;
- can support multitasking (e.g. writing a document while also talking to friends on msn; socialising with friends while also txting parents);
- need for brevity can be liberating – e.g. there aren't elaborate politeness routines in txting;
- can help to maintain interpersonal networks, but some (e.g. email) can also be used for official functions;
- can enable remote working for people;
- support minority interests, so people can feel connected;
- good for the environment as paper and transport costs saved (but electricity needed);
- broadcastable – i.e. can be used to communicate with large groups as well as individuals;

- editable, so writers can change and adapt text quickly;
- allow access to a wide variety of information sources, so people can be more active in their own learning;
- can be preserved as a permanent record, so can be reread;
- intertextual and multimodal – different tools can be combined (e.g. emails can carry attachments, txts can be added to photos sent via mobile phones, files can be transferred in msn);
- allow new ways of reading, new forms of literacy.

*Possible limitations*:
- amount of communication could be overwhelming (idea of an 'always on' society) and very time-consuming;
- mobility can be problematic if technology is not reliable;
- immediacy can encourage impulsive reactions when it might be better to delay;
- wide scope of publication entails issue of privacy and problem of interpretation by unknown and unpredictable audiences;
- asynchronous communication allows writers not to have to deal with impact of their communication, so writers can distance themselves;
- people can misrepresent themselves online;
- communication can easily be sent to the wrong person;
- difficulty of managing multitasking situations – e.g. do face-to-face or virtual friends take priority in social situations?;
- messages can be difficult to decode (e.g. abbreviations in txting);
- difficult to simulate the nuances of spoken voice, so can be misunderstood;
- ability to connect can be intrusive and aid criminality;
- broadcastability means that mistakes can be amplified;
- extent of information available can be overwhelming and encourage plagiarism;
- permanence of communication might not be welcome in some cases;
- ability to combine and transfer files could threaten individual privacy;
- new forms of literacy need to be understood and learned or some groups will be disadvantaged.

## Unit three, p. 21

You may well find that there is less abbreviation than you expected. Phone contracts offer generous txting parameters, so limitations of space and frequency are not so constraining as they were. Also, phones with key-boards are more common. Although space issues might not therefore be so important, speed might still be, so writers will still be trying to write messages quickly and concisely, whatever the nature of their phone.

Images might occur in your collection. Txters might be sharing images of their purchases, their pets, or their favourite sunset . . . Emoticons and other expressive features using non-alphabetic symbols might also occur, to represent aspects of non-verbal communication.

You might find that practical information and social arrangements account for many of your txts, as we use our phones to make plans that are flexible and subject to renegotiation. Phones are our personal accessories, so we use them for interpersonal, intimate messages: you may find that many messages express emotional connection (sometimes called 'affect'). This of course can include language with a strong loading of emotion – for example, swear words.

Many txts are likely to be multi-functional – for example, offering a salutation, suggesting a practical arrangement for a social event, or expressing friendship values. Participants are likely to play on shared understandings, use familiar names, and invoke their own 'voices' to replace a physical presence.

## Unit three (Text 3:1), p. 24

1    Thurlow's suggested features:

- shortenings: pos, wed, thurs, tho;
- contractions: remba, nek, wrk, jst, hw, lng, txt, piser, hme, cst, turnd, wud, nxt, sory, ths, bak, hd, turnd, wudve, hpe, nt, pisd;
- 'g' clipping: drivin, havin, setin, goin, flippin;
- other clippings: wher, wil, tho;
- acronyms and initialisms: V, b, u;
- letter/number homophones: 2, 1st, 4;
- non-conventional spellings: nitemare, anotha, sticka, dina;
- accent stylisation: wiv, flippin eck;
- non-alphabetic symbols: @ (for 'about'), !, x, xx;
- emoticons: ☺.

2    Other aspects typical of this type of communication:

- article deletion – e.g. 'wher is (the) pub?', 'near (the) minster';
- subject pronoun deletion – e.g. '(I) am on my bike thanks ☺', '(I am) on (my) way (I) need 2 get petrol 1st';
- informality between friends – e.g. mild swear words ('piser', 'flippin eck', 'pisd off').

3 and 4    Explanation for language features, and the txters' styles:

Speed and brevity can account for aspects of abbreviation, but Denise abbreviates much more extensively than Laura, producing quite a distinctive style. As predictive text has made the process of standardised writing much easier to achieve, it seems as though Denise really enjoys reshaping language to create her own mark of authorship. Laura's writing is much more standardised throughout.

Both writers express emotion about the event and affection towards each other.

## Unit three (Text 3:3), p. 32

Below are some of the textual details you may have picked up. Note that these lists are not definitive.

1    Relationship between the participants:

- Naming – the informal nature of this ('Nick', 'Rosie') shows that the participants know each other well.
- The fact that the participants feel no need to include greetings and closing items (e.g. 'regards', 'good luck with it') as the exchange develops, reinforces the idea that they share much 'common ground' (Clark, 1996).
- There are further aspects of the communication that suggest the participants are friends who share common ground: 'that reference' refers to an earlier conversation they had, showing that they communicate frequently; 'we have someone for the finance post' similarly refers back to a previous encounter; a place name ('bishopthorpe') and references to the media (*Friends*, *Guys and Gals*, *Wizard of Oz*) are assumed common knowledge.
- Humour and teasing are in evidence, showing, again, that participants know each other well. They jokingly accuse each other of worn-out attitudes ('typical man', 'oh linguist!' (Rosie

is a linguistics student)), but they take care to mark the non-serious nature of their accusations via expressive punctuation, particularly via exclamation marks, and via representation of a speech noise ('tut tut!!!!').

2    Frequent aspects of email communication:

- The gradual disappearance of the openings and closings of the messages as time goes on is also connected with the time frame of the communication: although a day elapses between the first and second messages, the final three all occur within a couple of hours on the same morning. This brings the messages closer to a sense of dialogue, giving them an interactive feel akin to spoken interaction, and taking them further away from the kinds of openings and closings familiar to us from the genre of formal written letters.

- Irregular capitalisation, omitted punctuation, and spellings and spaces left uncorrected (particularly by Rosie) show that this kind of informal email style can be based on different notions of correctness from the more formal kinds of writing seen in, for example, academic essays. Both writers omit articles ('the' and 'a'), verbs (particularly 'be' and 'have'), and subject pronouns ([I] 'will get it posted tomorrow'), bringing the style close to that of note-making. Early corpus-based studies of computer-based writing (e.g. Ferrara *et al.*, 1991; Collot and Belmore, 1996) often likened their data to notes and informal letters, citing the omissions above as characteristic of writing composed within time constraints. You may also have observed some of these same features in txt data you have analysed (although Shortis (2007) notes that txts allowing limited numbers of characters may not have room for multiple punctuation marks).

## Unit three (Text 3:5), p. 35

The themes covered in Elin's original email are:

- an opening 'how are you?' routine (with, perhaps, some recognition that she should have written earlier – 'time flies');
- comment about the weather;
- arrangements for meeting up, with several possibilities suggested, allowing Hannah many options and choices, including not meeting face to face at all;

- a closing, with some metalanguage (language about language), recognising her own politeness strategies, but also (via the smiley) suggesting she is amused by her own behaviour. 'Negative politeness' refers to the idea that we should not impose ourselves on others.

Hannah's reply is as follows:

- response to the weather comment, with a paralinguistic item (i.e. a feature suggesting a vocal effect, in this case weariness); this could be mirroring the emoticon strategy that Elin finished with;
- a positive response to the idea of meeting up, with a suggested arrangement;
- enthusiasm for the purpose of the meeting;
- an offer to do some forward planning (while using a negative politeness strategy to avoid seeming to dominate);
- exact mirroring of trailing dots and the same closing term.

Note, though, that Hannah does not mirror Elin's standard capitalisation, nor return her more formal opening of 'Dear X'.

## Unit 3 (Text 3:6), p. 37

Carrie's initial email has some marked informality – 'hi+first name' as a greeting/opening, use of lower case (apart from proper nouns), an abbreviated informal phrase ('fesses up', for 'confesses) and a mild swear word. The main semantic field is that of criminality, used in a humorous way: the 'crime' is not exactly a heinous one, so the criminal is constructed as more silly and thoughtless than calculating and evil ('some daft bugger has walked off with . . .'). The stolen item is playfully described as 'the magic pen'.

Patrick's reply matches Carrie's playful semantic field of criminality, using terms such as 'felony', 'amnesty' and 'herbert', and putting double quotes round the stolen item, the "pen". He goes further in his playfulness, painting a comic picture of a criminal trying to steal a large piece of furniture by hiding it under his braces. Patrick also mocks Carrie for being rather out of date ('Where HAVE you been!'), pointing out that he took some action, and playfully exaggerating how much this has all cost him personally (companies pay for this kind of technical equipment, not individual employees). He finishes by adding a mocking version of the regular institutional disclaimer, underlining its non-serious nature by including a smiley.

In strictly functional terms, Carrie's email is a complaint about things not working properly, and a request for remedial action. In equally functional terms, Patrick explains that he has sorted the problem. However, this email exchange is about considerably more than just this. These two colleagues co-construct a play scenario of criminality, humorously depicted and exaggerated, which enables them to share their common experience of working in an organisation where things go wrong and cause daily irritation and frustration. The organisational disclaimer at the end of Patrick's reply emphasises the difference between the rather pompous, official discourse that organisations force their employees to produce, and the creative exchange of these two individuals who signal their friendship and solidarity via their language choices.

## Unit three (Text 3:7), p. 40

- Participant A begins the proceedings by describing the item for sale, in slightly abbreviated form as you would in a traditional 'small ads' newspaper format (e.g. 'as new' and 'collect from central London').
- Participant B offers 50p less than the asking price, presumably hoping to knock A down, even though A said 'no offers'. But A is determined to stick to the asking price.
- B does not appear again.
- C uses a link to check the exact nature of the item – something that the online environment allows participants to do easily.
- A uses trailing dots and quotation marks to signal that whether someone regards the item as heavy rather depends on how much weight they can lift.
- While C thinks aloud about how the item could be transported, D arrives to join the bidding and C and D then get into a minor bidding competition. More deliberation about transportation by both C and D follows, finishing with D's suspicion that A is discussing the sale with someone else.
- This comment triggers quite a lengthy post by A, who reminds the participants that the forum is asynchronous so does not require constant presence (unlike a chatroom), then goes into considerable detail about the merits of the monitor. A also shows impatience with the discussion of transportation ('I don't mind whether you come by taxi, on foot, or by elephant').
- D offers a sort of apology by claiming that the comment about A's absence was meant as a joke.

- E then arrives and offers D another monitor for free, at which point D expresses gratitude via a loud protestation of love for E. C is now offered A's item and D acknowledges C's position as winner, while also recognising a stroke of personal fortune. A finishes with laughter and a smile, acknowledging a very good outcome.

This string of posts shows great delicacy by the participants and consideration of others' feelings. Even when A responds to the suggested accusation of attending to a bidder elsewhere, the reprimand is followed with a smiley to show no hard feelings. There are expressions of thanks and apologies, offers of help and detailed descriptions both of the item itself and of how best to manage its transportation. Each post serves to move the transaction along towards a group resolution.

## Unit four (Texts 4:4, 4:5 and 4:6), pp. 49/50

- Turntaking, seriality and adjacency

  Texts 4:4 and 4:5 have disrupted adjacency in their chatlogs. In 4:4, Anna tries to correct her misspelling of 'why' as 'wht', but then causes more confusion because her line 'I meant why !!' appears to rebuke Natalie for not having given enough of an explanation. In 4:5, Ryan's elliptical line 'talk to me' was intended as a reply to Lucy's 'do what?', but in its ellipted form Lucy takes it as an instruction and replies 'I am'.

  A focus on adjacency in real-time, multi-party writing reveals how important adjacency relationships are in interactive contexts. When lines are misplaced, it is also clear that many responses (second pair parts) could fit with more than one original expression (first pair part) in an adjacency pair. Equally clear is that, because of this potential ambiguity, the whole phenomenon of adjacency offers rich opportunities for play in this type of context.

- Length of turns

  It is noticeable that the more discursive interaction in Text 4:4 (and Text 4:2 in the main text) tends to feature lengthier turns compared with the episodes of play or (in Text 4:6) the exploration of how to represent a specific sound. Turn length is likely to be connected with the content and purpose of the interaction, so it would be interesting to compare different chatroom contexts where participants were using the tool for very different reasons.

- How far errors of spelling and other graphological aspects concern the participants

  There is evidence that participants are concerned when they have made a mistake that might cause a misunderstanding, but beyond that, correctness doesn't seem to be a priority. Having said that, most of the data here is written in standard English and do not feature many abbreviations. This could be connected with who the writers are, and the context of the interactions: the participants are university students, and they knew that their tutor would be able to read what they had written and therefore form an opinion of them.

- How aspects of voice are represented in writing

  Text 4:6 is a good example of two participants negotiating how a particular sound should best be represented in writing. Although differences between 'yeah' and 'yeay' are minimal in terms of spelling, the forms can be used to express some very different nuances of meaning.

- Language play

  There is much play here, which could, again, be connected with the nature of the participants. It could also be because, for these participants, writing in real time was a new phenomenon (it was before msn became popular), and play is a strategy for exploring one's environment. Think about how young children's play helps them to understand the world around them. We adults are no different when we encounter a new environment – language learning does not stop when we leave childhood.

## Unit five (Text 5:1), p. 61

Both writers are male.

## Unit seven (Texts 7:2 and 7:3), pp. 89/90

1   The headlines refer in dramatic terms to addictions and disease, via the words 'epidemic', 'drink' and 'dope'. Epidemic is, in particular, a word with strong connotations – of fast-spreading contagion, and a sense that we will soon be overwhelmed. The fact that addiction

**101**

and disease are being associated with txting shows journalists helping to foster a sense of moral panic about new forms of language use.

2    None of the headlines fit with their ensuing story particularly well. In 'English exam hit by epidemic of street language', the 'epidemic' turns out to be a report from the exam board Edexcel, where examiners say 'there was a surprising number of lapses' in standard English (hardly an epidemic). In 'Text-mad children turning to drink', there is no causal link made between txting and drinking. The article puts them together because both activities are seen as rebellious by teenagers (in Finland). In 'Texts "cause more harm than dope"', the article seems to be suggesting that txting preoccupies the brain more (while trying to do other tasks alongside it) than does smoking marijuana – hardly surprising, and actually quite reassuring. However, the headline made it seem as though txting would result in permanent brain damage, a meaning endorsed by the image of the teenager and the caption 'Dumbing down: Texting "can reduce your IQ"'.

3    The articles use a range of strategies to claim expertise and authority. The Text 7:3 quotes examiners' complaints about errors (but then, right at the end, acknowledges that some examiners saw an improvement in pupils' writing, which somewhat dilutes the force of the article). Halfway through the article, two completely different areas are introduced – boys' writing, and the national literacy strategy – to beef up what is in effect a fairly scant story. Other strategies to claim authority are the use of a list of examples of 'Street usage' to look a bit like an academic, factual source; and the phrase 'there is rising concern', which conveniently excuses the writer from having to say whose concern is rising.

The 'Text-mad children' article claims authority via phrases such as 'a report suggests' and 'psychologists say'. 'Texts "cause more harm than dope"' has the most specifically named sources of expertise, including a reference to who funded the research – Hewlett Packard, a major producer of office hardware and a company that might well have an interest in how people use new technologies in the workplace.

4    Research is quoted in the two articles in Text 7:2, but a reader would find it difficult to locate the research in question, as one gives just a journal title and the other just the research funder. In neither of these cases is it clear how the research has been done, or, indeed, what exactly has been researched.

5    The two articles in Text 7:2 use references to studies to create stories about txting as dangerous. The fact that the articles are about

children is significant, as the idea of children's vulnerability is often used to create a moral justification for writing articles. Academic researchers have noted that the thematic combination of children and technology is a classic basis for news stories stoking public fears (for example, Thurlow, 2003; Merchant, 2001).

The article in Text 7:3 is slightly different in that it introduces a concept – 'street language' – linking the idea of txting with other aspects of language use. It is very unclear what street language actually is. It sounds racy and real, but the list of examples includes not just txting (i, u, m8) but aspects of natural speech (wanna, shouda, gonna) and aspects of regional dialect (ain't). Presumably, in the writer's mind, street language is a kind of catch-all for language that is incorrect in some way, and associated with working-class or uneducated speakers, but the aspects of natural speech he lists can be heard every day in the language of highly educated figures such as politicians and academics.

# further reading

Andrejevic, M. (2007) *iSpy: Surveillance and Power in the Interactive Era*, Lawrence, KS: University of Kansas Press.

Chandler, D. (2007) *Semiotics: The basics*, London: Routledge.

Crystal, D. (2009) *Txtng: The Gr8 Db8*, Oxford: Oxford University Press.

Gane, N. and Beer, D. (2008) *New Media: The key concepts*, Oxford: Berg.

Gee, J.P. (2010) *How to Do Discourse Analysis: A toolkit*, London: Routledge.

Gee, J.P. and Hayes, E. (2011) *Language and Learning in the Digital Age*, London: Routledge.

Ito, M. (2010) *Hanging Out, Messing Around, and Geeking Out: Kids living and learning with new media*, Cambridge, MA: MIT Press.

# references

Access dates have been provided for websites to show exact date of cited information retrieval.

Baron, N. and Hård af Segerstad, Y. (2010) 'Cross-cultural patterns in mobile-phone use: public space and reachability in Sweden, the USA and Japan', *New Media and Society*, 12(13): 13–34.

Chandler, D. (2006) 'Identities under construction', in J. Maybin (ed.) *The Art of English*, Maidenhead: Open University Press.

Clark, H. (1996) *Using Language*, Cambridge: Cambridge University Press.

Collot, M. and Belmore, N. (1996) 'Electronic language: a new variety of English', in S. Herring (ed.) *Computer-mediated Communication: Linguistic, social and cross-cultural perspectives*, Amsterdam: John Benjamins, pp. 13–28.

Condon, S. and Cech, C. (2002) 'If you can read this, you're a cyborg: turn structure in virtual interaction', paper presented at the GURT 2002: Georgetown University Roundtable on Linguistics, Washington DC.

Crandall, J. (2007) 'Showing'. Available online at http://jordancrandall.com/showing/index.html (accessed 15 January 2011).

Crystal, D. (2001) *Language and the Internet*, Cambridge: Cambridge University Press.

Ferrara, K., Brunner, H. and Whittemore, G. (1991) 'Interactive written discourse as an emergent register', *Written Communication*, 8(1): 8–34.

Findahl, O. (2009) 'The young and the internet in Sweden 2009'. Available online at www.worldinternetproject.net/#reports (accessed 18 January 2011).

Forensic Linguistics Institute (2010) 'Recent cases'. Available online at www.thetext.co.uk (accessed 18 January 2011).

Gee, J.P. (1990) *Social Linguistics and Literacies: Ideology in discourses*, Bristol, PA: Falmer Press.

Giles, H. and St Clair, R. (eds) (1979) *Language and Social Psychology*, London: Basil Blackwell.

Goffman, E. (1997) *The Goffman Reader* (eds C. Lemert and A. Brauman), Oxford: Blackwell.

Greenwood, L. (2009) 'Africa's mobile banking revolution', *BBC News*, 12 August. Available online at http://news.bbc.co.uk/1/hi/business/8194241.stm (accessed 18 January 2011).

**105**

Hackforth, R. (1972) *Plato's Phaedrus*, Cambridge: Cambridge University Press.

Hansell, S. (2009) 'The broadband gap: why do they have more fiber?', *The New York Times*, 12 March. Available online at http://bits.blogs.nytimes.com/2009/03/12/the-broadband-gap-why-do-they-have-more-fiber/?scp=2&sq=slow%20broadband&st=cse (accessed 18 January 2011).

Jenkins, H. (2010) 'Google and the search for the future', *Wall Street Journal*, 14 August. Available online at http://online.wsj.com/article/SB10001424052748704901104575423294099527212 (accessed 18 January 2011).

Keen, A. (2007) *The Cult of the Amateur: How today's internet is killing our culture*, New York: Doubleday.

Leadbeater, C. (2008a) *We-think: Mass innovation, not mass production*, London: Profile Books.

Leadbeater, C. (2008b) 'Welcome to we-think: mass innovation, not mass production'. Available online at www.wethinkthebook.net/home.aspx (accessed 18 January 2011).

Lyon, D. (2007) *Surveillance Studies: An overview*, Cambridge: Polity.

Manovich, L. (2008) 'The practice of everyday (media) life'. Available online at www.manovich.net/TEXTS_07.HTM (accessed 18 January 2011).

Merchant, G. (2001) 'Teenagers in cyberspace: an investigation of language use and language change in internet chatrooms', *Journal of Research in Reading*, 24(3): 293–306.

Mitchell, W.J. (2003) *Me++: The cyborg self and the networked city*, Cambridge, MA: MIT Press.

Naisbitt, J. (1982) *Megatrends*, New York: Warner.

Nakagawa, E. and Unebasami, K. (2008) *I Can Has Cheezeburger?: A Lolcat colleckshun*, New York: Gotham Books.

O'Reilly, T. (2005) 'What is Web 2.0: design patterns and business models for the next generation of software'. Available online at http://oreilly.com/web2/archive/what-is-web-20.html (accessed 18 January 2011).

Scollon, R. (2001) 'Multimodal discourses', plenary presentation at GURT: Georgetown University Round Table on Languages and Linguistics, Washington DC.

Sellen, A. and Harper, R. (2001) *The Myth of the Paperless Office*, Cambridge, MA: MIT Press.

Shirky, C. (2000) 'RIP the consumer 1900–1999'. Available online at www.shirky.com/writings/consumer.html (accessed 18 January 2011).

Shortis, T. (2007) 'Revoicing txt', in S. Postequillo, M. Esteve and M. Gea-Valor (eds) *The Texture of Internet: Netlinguistics in progress*, Cambridge: Cambridge Scholars Publishing.

Thurlow, C. (2003) 'Generation Txt? The sociolinguistics of young people's text-messaging', *Discourse Analysis Online*. Available online at http://extra.shu.ac.uk/daol/articles/v1/n1/a3/thurlow2002003-t.html (accessed 18 January 2011).

Thurlow, C., Lengel, L. and Tomic, A. (2004) *Computer Mediated Communication: Social interaction and the internet*, London: Sage.

Tryhorn, C. (2009) 'Nice talking to you . . . mobile phone use passes milestone', *The Guardian*, 3 March. Available online at www.guardian.co.uk/technology/2009/mar/03/mobile-phones1 (accessed 18 January 2011).

Turnage, A.K. (2007) 'Email flaming behaviors and organizational conflict', *Journal of Computer-Mediated Communication*, 13(1): 43–59. doi: 10.1111/j.1083-6101.2007.00385.x.

Werry, C. (1996) 'Linguistic and interactional features of internet relay chat', in Herring, S (ed.) *Computer-mediated Communication: Linguistic, social and cross-cultural perspectives*, Amsterdam: John Benjamins, pp. 47–63.

Wikipedia (2010) 'Wikipedia: about'. Available online at http://en.wikipedia.org/wiki/Wikipedia:About (accessed 18 January 2011).

YouTube (2010) 'YouTube fact sheet'. Available online at www.youtube.com/t/fact_sheet (accessed 18 January 2011).

# index of terms

This is a form of combined glossary and index. Listed below are some of the key terms used in the book, together with brief definitions for purposes of reference. The page references will normally take you to the first use of the term in the book, where it will be shown in bold.

**addressivity**  47
The process of using a term of address (for example, a personal name) to indicate the intended audience for the communication.

**adjacency**  46
The positioning of elements in an interaction so that one follows from another. For example, greetings are nearly always reciprocated in an adjacency pair.

**affordances**  15
The things that a communication system can enable users to do.

**asynchronous**  38
Describes communication that is not reliant on participants being present or online at the same time.

**bots**  53
Computer programmes that are used for routine, repetitive tasks.

**bricolage**  51
A term first used by Claude Levi Strauss to refer to the idea of artistic assembly in creative tasks.

**chain**  27
As used in this book, the phenomenon of linking seen in online texts such as emails and discussion forum posts.

**chatlog**  45
A written record of what participants produce in a real-time online interaction.

**citizen journalists**  66
Writers who are not professionals but who use social media to produce and disseminate their own interpretation of events.

**constraints**  14
The things that a communication system can prevent users from doing.

**critique**  77
To stand back and analyse a statement or idea in detail.

**cultural lag**  57
The phenomenon whereby technology moves more quickly than we can manage to adapt to it.

**demographics**  70
Statistical information on a particular population or group within a population, such as gender, age, occupation, nationality, etc.

**dialogic** 21
The quality of interactivity, being like dialogue.

**digital double** 55
Electronic profile of an individual that combines information gathered by others with information that individuals themselves contribute online. Synonyms: data double, software self and digital persona.

**discourse** 36
A system of representation, related references and associated understandings that frame an object, event or person in a particular way. Sometimes linguists will use the phrase 'discourse analysis' to refer to the detailed analysis of an extended stretch of text on one occasion, while social scientists may focus more widely on ways of talking and writing across whole cultures (this is termed 'Discourse with a capital D', by Gee (1990)).

**flaming** 36
Angry outbursts from online communicators, using capital letters or other devices.

**folksonomy** 64
A form of collaborative categorisation where individuals 'tag' content with any relevant keywords. It is an important development that makes social media databases, such as YouTube, searchable. It is useful because it allows for a wide variety of connections and associations rather than rigidly putting items into one category or folder.

**forensic linguistics** 21
A branch of applied linguistics that focuses on crime and legal issues.

**framing** 33
As used in the context of writing online, the process of chopping up text and responding to others' communication in sections.

**genre** 15
A type of text with its own distinctive characteristics.

**hybrid** 22
A combination, or mixture. Online communication is often seen as a mixture of spoken and written characteristics.

**identity** 36
The sense we have of ourselves and others as individuals and group members, and the 'story' or version of the individual or group that is portrayed and perceived.

**idiolect** 21
An individual's distinctive uses of language.

**interactivity** 22
The quality of give and take characterising communication that occurs in real time.

**limitations** 15
Synonymous with constraints, the things that a communication system can prevent users from doing.

**LOLcat** 72
A photo of a cat with a humorous caption created collaboratively online, which is uploaded to a social media database such as 'I Can Haz Cheezeburger'. The prefix 'LOL', which originally in netspeak was an abbreviation of 'Laugh out loud', is now applied to multiple versions of an online website with tagged photos with humorous captions.

**109**

**LOLspeak** 72

Sometimes referred to as 'kitty pidgin', a humorous language variation commonly associated with online websites such as LOLcats or other varieties of 'Lols'. Common characteristics are misspellings, grammatical errors, and reference to a number of phrases and names drawn from other popular internet and video game trends.

**maxims** 22

Ideas or principles that underlie activity.

**metalanguage** 47

The use of language that refers to language itself. For example, when someone says 'to cut a long story short', they are using language to describe their own linguistic behaviour.

**multimodality** 13

Using more than one mode of communication at the same time – for example, written text and image.

**non-linear** 33

Refers to the idea that a text can be read in a way other than in a line-by-line fashion. For example, webpages can be connected via links that occur at various points in the text.

**paralinguistic** 23

Relates to aspects of communication beyond the actual words used. For example, facial expression or tone of voice in speech, or the quality of paper or screen resolution in other media.

**phishing** 30

Criminal attempts to acquire sensitive information about individuals, such as their bank account details.

**phonological** 23

Relating to the sounds of speech.

**porous** 33

As used about online communication, refers to the idea that texts have 'holes' in them in the sense of being able to be clicked through to get to other sites.

**posts** 38

As used about online communication, messages that are put up in discussion forums or on social networking sites for public viewing.

**premodifier** 48

A word or phrase that comes before a noun or verb and adds detail.

**presentational culture** 56

A cultural shift where individuals increasingly value visibility over privacy. As watching others becomes a form of entertainment (reality television and social networking sites), individuals invite being watched and increasingly publish more and more of their personal details.

**prosodic** 48

Related to the sounds of connected speech, such as intonation patterns.

**prosumers** 64

A term that blends 'producers' and 'consumers', describing internet use where individuals are both consuming and producing their own content. An example would be bloggers.

**prosumption** 66

Related to 'prosumers', referring to the blended act of production and consumption, typified by blogs or user-generated content sites such as Fanfiction.net.

**repertoire**  21
A range of available options. As used here, a range of possible styles that communicators could adopt.

**representation**  1
The way people and things appear to be, i.e. the stories that we tell about the world around us.

**semantic fields**  51
Areas of language use relating to common themes or topics, for example, the language of cookery or fishing.

**seriality**  46
One element occurring after another. This can be contrasted with adjacency, which describes one element connected with another (but which could be removed in time or distance, such as displaced lines in a chatlog).

**SMS**  15
An abbreviation of Short Message System, or txts.

**social media**  55
Media, typically those characterised as a part of Web 2.0, in which social interaction is an encouraged key component. Social networking websites such as Twitter, YouTube, etc. are key examples.

**social networking sites (SNSs)**  15
Online environments where individuals publish information about themselves that is viewable by chosen others. Many SNSs are multimodal, allowing participants to leave messages asynchronously but also to interact in real time when both parties are online simultaneously.

**social sorting**  59
'Processes of selection, inclusion and exclusion' to develop schemas of 'classification and categorization' (Lyon, 2007: 204), often aided by technological devices and the development of complex databases.

**sociolinguistics**  22
An area of language study that examines the relationship between language use and social groups.

**stylistic**  30
Related to choices of style in language use. For example, the same thing or idea can be described via informal or formal vocabulary, such as 'try' versus 'endeavour'.

**synchronous**  45
Describes communication that occurs in real time.

**tagging**  51
As used in this book, the process of creating a folksonomy by applying various keywords to a particular item online (photo, story, video, etc.) to enable categorisation and searchability.

**turntaking**  47
An aspect of real-time communication whereby people cooperate with each other to maintain the participative nature of interactions.

**txting**  15
The process of composing, sending and receiving messages via mobile phone.

**Web 2.0**  51
The common term to refer to the second phase of the internet, beginning in the early 2000s, distinguished from earlier use of the internet by a focus on collaboration, interactivity and user-generated content.

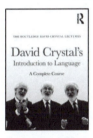

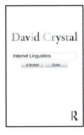